PTSD

Understanding and Recovery

Rosalind Townsend

POMEGRANATE · PRESS·

Acknowledgements

PTSD Resolution is pleased to have been able to support the production of this book, and to receive a percentage of the proceeds of the sales.

"Ros Townsend and PTSD Resolution gave me the best treatment I ever had. They made me feel like a person again."
Gunner, Royal Artillery, Northern Ireland veteran

Thanks also go to **The 'Lest We Forget' Association** for their generous sponsorship.

Cover illustration and other artwork © Sofi Smith.

ISBN 978-1-907242-67-0

British Library Cataloguing-in-Publication data
A catalogue record for this book is available from the British Library.

Published by Pomegranate Press
South Chailey, Lewes, Sussex BN8 4QB
email: pomegranatepress@aol.com
website: www.pomegranate-press.co.uk
Printed by 4Edge, Hockley, Essex SS5 4AD

Contents

Foreword

*by **Gordon Turnbull**,*
Lead trauma consultant, Nightingale Hospital;
consultant psychiatrist, Chester University.

I am delighted to have been given the opportunity to write the foreword to this book. This is not only because I've learned new things from it, which I have. Having developed a special fascination for traumatic stress reactions during my experience spanning more than four decades in internal medicine, neurology and psychiatry in the Royal Air Force and then in civilian practice, it has been stimulating to learn new things about the subject.

But there are other reasons for me to have enjoyed this book so much. For example, I have long debated (with myself and with others working in the field) whether PTSD represents an illness state or 'a normal reaction to abnormal events' which has 'got stuck'.

This has never been resolved, but Rosalind Townsend's insights have pushed me powerfully towards my preferred concept that the PTSD phenomenon is more likely to be part of the 'human condition' than a disease. This did not occur to me on a whim. I noticed it first in some of the RAF Mountain Rescue troops who were subsequently involved in the 1988 Lockerbie Air Disaster, and whom I had got to know in Cyprus when I was their team 'doc'. I had the strong impression that they were very tough, resilient and experienced: the immediate impact of Lockerbie had changed them, as they wrestled with the impact of a catastrophic event, but I did not consider them to have developed an illness. I suspect that Rosalind Townsend has had similar experiences. As a clinician one has to learn things in the clinic room with eye, ear and focused mind and not just from textbooks. A psychiatrist/psychologist needs to have the eye of an owl, the ear of an elephant and the mindset of David Attenborough.

That doesn't make suffering from PTSD any the less unpleasant, but it can lead to enhancement of one's survival skills and becomes a positive force. If PTSD could be recognised as a 're-adjustment of mind, body and spirit' following traumatic shock, leading to the potential for recovery and personal growth, would that not provide survivors more incentive to engage with recovery strategies than the current attitude of hoping to recover from a psychiatric illness? If successful recovery from PTSD could cause the ghosts of 'lack of moral fibre', 'cowardice' and the like to creep back into their dark historical roots, then it could achieve the greatest goal possible in modern psychiatry, the eradication of that biggest obstacle to recovery, *stigma*.

From the outset, *PTSD: Understanding and Recovery* tackles these issues, correctly perceiving them to be at the core of the subject. The book takes up the challenge of explaining why some individuals develop PTSD and others don't. It gives a modern explanation of how the neurobiological mechanisms responsible for information-processing and memory adapt to the impact of trauma. The functional adaptations of other parts of the mind and the body are explained in more physiological rather than pathological terms. The typical symptoms of PTSD are the manifestations of the struggle for restored balance of body and brain function.

World War I may have punched the phenomenon of trauma reactions such as shellshock into public consciousness, but it took World War II and Vietnam to build the necessary momentum for PTSD to enter the psychiatric classification systems. It has become the most-researched medical condition of all time so far, and has provided an impetus towards understanding other neuro-psychiatric conditions as well.

Readers of this book will reflect how the definition of Criterion A for the brand new 'PTSD' in the *Diagnostic and Statistical Manual of the American Psychiatric Association*, third edition 1980 (an attempt to define what a traumatic event is) has changed from 'an event beyond usual human experience' to a new definition at each of the DSM revisions. This has extended the value of PTSD as a construct beyond military experiences and major disasters to assist the survivors of trauma in everyday situations, as well as those in the caring professions and in the law.

Why the ear of the elephant? Well, it helps to find the trauma element in patients with complex presentations such as pain when they answer the question 'Is there anything you have experienced in your life that still haunts you and distresses you?' And it's never too late to detect PTSD because it can be treated at any stage in life.

Congratulations to Rosalind Townsend for writing this book. My hope is that it will be widely read by survivors and therapists and that it will help to eradicate the hidden enemy– *stigma*.

Gordon Turnbull

"We read to know we are not alone."

C.S. Lewis

This book is for, and because of, the bravest people who I have ever had the honour to meet and work with – those people who, in the face of the real terror and distress that PTSD can cause, still seek to recover, help others and make a life that works. People like Mike, Steve, Smudge, Rich, Norm, Mac, Bob, Trevor, Chris, Kelley, Ian, Rachel, Mark and many, many others . . . the list goes on.

It is also dedicated to Jack, who in so many ways has taught and given me more than anyone, and for my children who have an understanding, that goes way beyond their years, of the work that is so important to me.

My sincere thanks must also go to John Halker and Julian Penton, colleagues who I am also lucky enough to consider good friends, who have supported me, my work and the writing of this book in so many ways.

And it is finally for Joe, who brought so much to my attention when I needed it most, and whose voice always goes with me. Thank you.

Rosalind Townsend, Cornwall, 2018

"This book should be printed in hardback –
and used to hit certain people over the head with!"
MW, ex RN

PART 1

Understanding PTSD

What is PTSD?

PTSD stands for Post Traumatic Stress Disorder.

The term PTSD is commonly used to describe a range of physical and emotional symptoms that people may experience following a traumatic event – and which sometimes do not emerge until years later.

PTSD was first recognised in any real sense following the return of soldiers from the First World War and has, in its time, been known as soldier's heart, shell shock, battle fatigue and combat stress. In more recent years many people have been told that they are 'ill' or that it is a 'disease'.

For many years there has also been a misconception (which persists in many circles) that PTSD can develop *only* following some kind of military incident. This is simply not the case. *Any* traumatic event, be it military or civilian, given the right set of circumstances, can become a catalyst for a post-traumatic reaction. Indeed, many of the veterans I have worked with undoubtedly have PTSD but it relates solely or largely to an event or events in their personal or civilian life.

This guide will explain how the latest understandings recognise PTSD, most usefully, as the inappropriate and persistent firing of an essential and normal response in our system: the fight-or-flight response. This firing (and the knock-on effects of it) occur in response to a traumatic or, often, a series of traumatic or distressing events.

This understanding has led many of those who work most successfully in this field in a military setting to re-name it PTSI (Post-Traumatic Stress Injury) or PTSR (Post-Traumatic Stress Reaction). In this guide, we will refer to it simply as PTS (Post-Traumatic Stress), reflecting the fact that it is now widely recognised as a reaction to a traumatic event or events – rather than a 'disorder'.

Part 1 of this guide will give you an understanding of:

• The particular symptoms associated with PTS, why these symptoms occur, and the 'purpose' they serve

• How these symptoms can, without the right understanding and support, lead to a person feeling that their life is spiralling rapidly out of control

Part 2 of this guide will:

• Introduce you to specific tools and coping strategies that you can begin using right away to ensure that you are able to begin taking control of your life again

• Point you to further sources of accurate and useful information and support

What makes something a 'trauma'?

A trauma is any event which is life-threatening, highly distressing or, importantly, that we *believe* to be life-threatening or highly distressing.

Such events could include:

• Being mugged, raped or attacked

• Rail accidents, or car or plane crashes

• Natural disasters

• Physical, sexual or psychological abuse or torture

• Having a heart attack or distressing medical procedure

• A difficult childbirth

• Being involved in combat or violent conflict

For military personnel or members of the emergency services, the likelihood of experiencing one or several traumatic events, especially if engaged in active service, is high.

Does everyone develop long-term difficulties after a trauma?

No. Following any traumatic event, it is natural to feel extreme emotions: shock or distress, guilt, sadness or anger – or to feel 'numb'. The majority of people, however, are able to gradually process whatever has occurred, and move on from it.

About 20 per cent, however, go on to develop a troublesome post-traumatic stress reaction. This can occur in the weeks and months following the trauma, or can only become apparent many years later – almost always during, or following, a period of increased stress of one kind or another.

What are the symptoms?

All the following symptoms are part of the cluster that often leads to a diagnosis of PTSD:

• **Flashbacks and nightmares**, which can be so realistic that you feel as though you are actually re-living the experience over again

• **Avoidance** of any situation, place, person, or object that might remind you of the traumatic situation

• Being constantly 'on guard' – often know as **hypervigilance**

• Poor quality of **sleep**

• Persistent feelings of **fear** or **anxiety**

• **Panic attacks**

• Irritability and inappropriate outbursts of **anger**

• Difficulty in feeling a **'normal' range of emotions** such as love, caring, or appropriate sadness or anger

• Feelings of **low mood** (sometimes diagnosed as depression)

• **Withdrawal** from activities and relationships that once gave you pleasure

• Faulty coping strategies to escape from the difficulties such as **comfort eating**, **excessive physical exercise**, or self-medication with **alcohol** or **drugs**

• **Poor memory**

• **Difficulty concentrating, 'thinking straight' or making decisions**

• A fragmented **'sense of self'**

Why some and not others?

How do some people walk away from horrifying experiences, seemingly unharmed, whilst others go on to experience severe difficulties? Is it due to a 'weakness' or, as used to be mistakenly thought, a 'lack of moral fibre'?

Firstly, it is now understood that we all have the potential to develop a post-traumatic stress reaction. This potential is the price we pay for having a fully functioning in-built survival response: the fight-or-flight mechanism.

Secondly, there are several factors that have been consistently observed to make it more likely that an individual will experience difficulties following a traumatic incident:

• If the situation in which you are involved is particularly horrific, involves children, or causes many deaths or mutilation

• If you have no means of escape or taking action during the trauma

• If you experience more than one trauma (post-traumatic stress is cumulative)

• If your stress levels (due to other ongoing stressors) are high before the trauma

• If your stress levels (due to other ongoing stressors) are high after the trauma

• If you have a good imagination

Almost everyone who develops a problematic post-traumatic stress reaction does so because some of these factors have come together in a 'perfect storm'.

How does it happen?

"Understanding what was going on made it all make sense,
all the bits that had just been happening suddenly linked up.
It didn't make it better right away but it took some of the fear
away and was a good first step." AJ

In order to understand what happens to cause a post-traumatic stress reaction and then, most importantly, how to begin to put things right, it is useful to understand some basic facts about the way our brain and physiological systems work when they are functioning well.

Although the study of the brain and our physiology can be endlessly complicated, understanding enough to be able to make sense of the symptoms of post traumatic stress, and then to be able find ways of working with them to improve a current situation, is happily not too complex at all.

The brain as an office

Many of the veterans and civilians with PTS who I have worked with over the years have found it very useful to begin building an understanding of the brain by thinking of it in terms of an office.[i]

When we are calm, our brain can be thought of as being like a well-run office.

The Secretary
anterior cingulate gyrus

The Boss `YOU`
pre-frontal neo-cortex

The Filing Cabinet
hippocampus

Security Guard
amygdala

Our rational brain (the pre-frontal neo-cortex) is the boss in charge. This is the part of the brain that can, in simple terms, make decisions, organise and structure, and is involved in creating our working memory.

Within the office, the secretary (the anterior cingulate gyrus) deals with information incoming through our senses, and decides which bits should be filed, and which prioritised and sent through to the boss.

Information is stored in, and can be easily retrieved from, the hippocampus – our personal filing cabinet.

At the door of our office is a primitive part of the brain called the amygdala. This can be thought of as our brain's 'security guard'. When we are calm he is very well-trained, coolly scanning the environment, and is the first to be aware of any incoming information. Although on the lookout for danger, he is not on red-alert or constantly expecting the worst.

Our brain functions like this when levels of stress hormones (such as cortisol and adrenaline) are low in our system. When our brain is functioning in this state we have the ability to think clearly, make good decisions and keep things on track; we have the resilience to cope with the inevitable ups and downs of day-to-day life.

Trauma occurs

At some time or another, however, almost all of us will experience a life-threatening, extremely distressing or 'traumatic' situation. This is when something called the fight-or-flight response kicks in to help us to survive.

The diagram below, known as a LIFE diagram,[ii] illustrates clearly how our system responds to such a situation.

The cartoon faces up the side show the level of stress hormones such as cortisol in our system. The darkest red zone at the very top, next to the face indicating extreme distress, shows the level at which a full firing of the fight-or-flight response is triggered. Across the bottom are the life events we might encounter during a day.

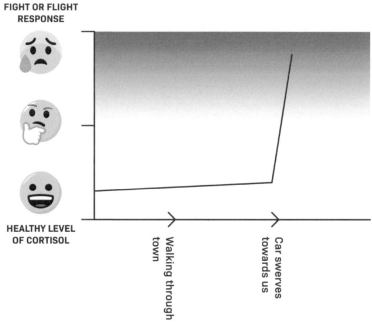

In this example, a normal start to the day is followed by a huge burst of cortisol flooding our system and pushing us up into fight-or-flight mode when, while walking through town, a vehicle suddenly swerves towards us on the pavement.

The fight/flight response

In order that we have the best chance of surviving the situation and getting out of the way of the car, our body and our brain undergo a series of dramatic changes all designed to make us as fast, strong and effective as possible. Sequences of nerve cells fire, and chemical messengers (like adrenaline and cortisol) are released into our bloodstream.

These cause:

• Our respiratory (breathing) rate to increase to get extra oxygen on board in case we have to run away or fight

The Secretary
anterior cingulate gyrus

The Boss YOU
pre-frontal neo-cortex

The Filing Cabinet
hippocampus

Security Guard
amygdala

• Our heart rate to increase so that extra blood can be pumped around our system

• Our digestive system to shut down as blood is diverted away from it and directed to our muscles and limbs, which require extra energy and fuel for running or fighting

•Our pupils to dilate, sharpening our sight and awareness

• Our impulses to quicken and our perception of pain to diminish

• Our body to sweat, in order that we don't overheat during the vigorous activity of running or fighting.

Most importantly, in our understanding of PTS, access to the upper, 'thinking' parts of the brain (the boss, secretary and filing cabinet) are shut down and the primitive amygdala (the security guard) takes charge, so that it can take life-saving decisions in a split second.

Why?

The burning question at this point, and certainly the burning question for me when I first encountered this bit of information, was *why*? Why on earth, when faced with potentially the most difficult situation of our lives, have we been wired as human beings to lose access to the majority of our intelligence and the upper part of our brain – the very bits that might, it would seem, help us deal with it successfully?

The answer is actually quite simple. The upper part of the brain, the bit that contains the boss, the secretary and the filing cabinet works, in neurological terms, much, much slower than the primitive security guard (amygdala). The last thing we want is for a slow, rational boss, as the car hurtles towards us, to start questioning whether it is a stunt for a film or whether the driver will have time to brake: what we want is an incredibly fast-acting part of the brain to give us the strength and speed to get out of danger immediately. And this is exactly what happens. The security guard seizes control of the brain in order that he can force us to take speedy action to survive.

He also, in case we do survive the situation and ever encounter a similar one in future, takes in all the information about that dangerous situation that he can, and stores it as a set of simple templates for danger. A red car, the squealing sound of brakes, a set of traffic lights, perhaps, or a blue sky overhead.

As we then take immediate and often physical action to keep ourselves safe (in this case jumping out of the path of the swerving car), we use up the fight-or- flight response as it was designed to be used. The extra oxygen, the increased blood circulation, the sweating and so on do their job. Once out of danger, our system begins to calm down.

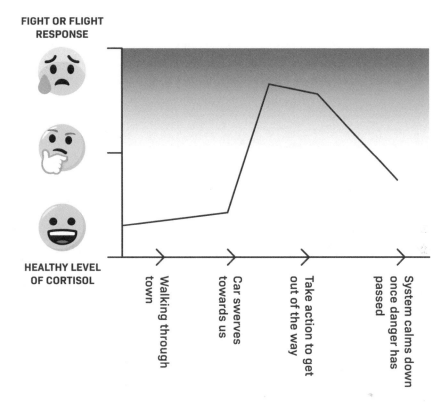

Importantly, as the levels of stress hormones begin to drop and our system returns to normal, access to our thinking brain becomes possible. Our hippocampus (filing cabinet) and security guard can begin to communicate. This means that context and detail can be added to the simple 'danger templates' of the trauma memory, allowing us to process the event as something that occurred at a specific time in the past, in a specific place, due to a specific car and a specific set of circumstances.

What disrupts the process in PTS?

A traumatised person can feel as though they live 'in a private hell: hyper alert, terrorised by an invisible mental wound, helplessly in thrall to a powerful emotional memory of a life-threatening event or series of events'.[iv]

The problems occur if, for some reason, stress levels remain high after the event and chemical messengers continue to block access to the upper-brain so that crucial additional information and detail relating to the trauma cannot be passed from the boss (pre-frontal neocortex) and filing cabinet (hippocampus) to the security guard (amygdala). This means that the brain continues to rely on overly simplistic and thus often inaccurate information relating to the trauma.

This continued block is especially likely to occur if levels of emotional arousal at the time of the trauma are high because:

• It is a particularly distressing situation

• We are already very stressed due to difficult and on-going life circumstances

• It is the most recent of many traumas

• We experience the situation in 'freeze'

Freeze is the third option available if, for some reason, we cannot fight or fly (i.e. take action to make things safe or run away). In this state, it can feel as though time slows down, or as though we are experiencing the event as an observer (sometimes termed 'dissociation').

In this state the templates for danger are encoded particularly deeply into the amygdala.[iii] This inability to 'fight' or 'fly' is why a less 'time specific' event, such as watching helpless as a relative dies over a period of months, can be as traumatic as a dramatic and horrific car accident, and can equally result in symptoms of PTS.

When the upper brain remains inaccessible, and communication between it and the security guard cannot take place, no specifics or details can be added to the memory to allow it to be processed at a higher level: details like, for example, the fact that the car was an Audi, driven by a particular drunken driver in wet conditions – or, for a soldier, that the loud bang that quite rightly sent them into fight-flight mode occurred during a fire-fight in a war zone.

Working alone to keep us safe, the amygdala simply stores 'red car' – or, in the soldier's case, 'loud bang' – as a pattern to be on guard against in future. It also stores other simplistic information associated with the traumatic situation that might in reality have nothing to do with the danger itself:

• That a woman in a red coat or with brown hair was standing nearby when the 'loud bang' occurred;

• That a certain smell was in the air

• That there were tall buildings lining the street where the crash happened

With such simple templates to rely on, it is little wonder that after the event is over, as our amygdala (security guard) constantly scans the environment on a sub-conscious level for danger, looking for things that might resemble those templates and thus pose a threat, it often makes faulty pattern matches.

This is why *all* loud bangs (even a car back-firing) can cause terror and distress; why the smell of fuel, even if we know we are in a filling station, might make us feel uncomfortable; why a person dressed in a certain colour or with a certain hair colour brings on overwhelming feelings of panic; or why we feel a rationally inexplicable urge to get away if we find ourselves in a street lined with tall buildings.

In PTS, so many innocent triggers cause terror that the affected person lives in a permanent state of fear and constantly feels 'on guard' – however many times they might try to reassure themselves rationally that an environment is 'safe'. Each time a pattern match is made to some aspect of the original trauma, the fight-or-flight state is triggered, the security guard takes over, and access to the upper brain is shut down. It is as if, to return to the office scenario, the security guard has been put on a state of heightened alert and then given a set of very simply and poorly sketched mugshots of people that he must treat as a substantial threat if they approach the building.

The more stressed the person is, the less detail is included in these sketches (hence the fact that many sufferers have 'good days' where they can cope with more, and 'bad days' where everything seems to trigger a response). With only the rough outline of a woman with fair hair or a man in a hat to go on, and no further details to identify them, it is entirely understandable that such a security guard would be jumping at all of the many people entering the building who could fit that description.

But most of those people that he reacted to would not be the correct man in a hat or woman with fair hair – most of them would be false alarms, just as most of the loud bangs heard by a soldier recently returned from Afghan to a sleepy village in Cambridgeshire, or most red cars seen afterwards by the driver involved in the horrific crash, would be. But because the security guard does not have enough information to tell the difference he still prepares the body to fight or fly. And with nothing to fight or run away from, the body's preparations result in the distressing physical symptoms of anxiety, fear or a panic attack; cause irritability, or explode in an inappropriate anger outburst.

What is more, anything that is then experienced in that state of distress is *also* stored by the amygdala as a template for danger – so the shop in which you had the panic attack, or the activity you were doing at the time, can also become things which trigger the fight-or-flight state inappropriately. This explains why these symptoms seem so often to cascade through a life, with more and more places or things feeling unsafe. Indeed, in the extreme, it can result in a person finding it increasingly difficult to feel 'safe' at all outside of their home or a particular room.

A traumatised soldier I worked with recently experienced a major panic attack, completely out of the blue it seemed, when he went for a walk on a beach with his family. It was, by all accounts, a lovely day and he couldn't understand why feelings of complete terror had suddenly overwhelmed him. It was only when we were talking about the incident afterwards that he realised that the original trauma he experienced had been in a sandy desert environment. It then immediately became clear that his amygdala had completely mismatched the sand of a Cornish beach to that other sand in a far away, war-torn country and sent messages throughout his system to tell him that he was in extreme danger.

Moving forward

"I struggle switching off at all . . . I haven't really slept for the last three years. I'm not good in crowds. The other day me wife dropped a frying pan and I hit the roof and it took me hours to calm down." PS

If we have been traumatised in this way, it can feel as though our life is out of control. We may become angry or fearful at the slightest thing and sometimes, for seemingly no real reason at all, be plagued by terrifying dreams or flashbacks, as the amygdala (our security guard) mistakenly reacts to any reminder of the situation and takes us 'right back there'. We may experience persistent and intrusive thoughts about the event; we may be unable to visit places or undertake activities that most people take for granted.

A first step along the road to recovery is understanding that all these symptoms are either:

• Linked to the fight-or-flight response firing inappropriately;

• An attempt to avoid this firing from happening;

or

• The knock-on effects of both of the above.

Panic attacks explained

A panic attack is one of the most distressing and terrifying non-life threatening experiences that a human being can have.

It occurs when our body makes dramatic preparations for fight-or-flight but there is nothing really to fight or fly from. The fight-or-flight response is then 'all dressed up with nowhere to go', and we are left in our armchair or in the supermarket having subconsciously taken a load of extra oxygen on board (making us feel breathless), with our heart pumping extra blood furiously round our system and our hands trembling and sweating, swamped by the most horrendous feelings of fear and distress – and perhaps experiencing an overwhelming urge to 'escape'.

Understanding exactly what a panic attack is, and what each symptom is, can be the first step towards coping with them effectively, and eventually leaving them behind.

Three key facts about a panic attacks:

A panic attack is the fight/flight response firing inappropriately.

A panic attack is of no more danger to a physically healthy individual than any other form of vigorous work-out for the heart. (It is always best, however, if you experience unexpected physical symptoms to get them checked out by the doctor. Once you have been told that the unpleasant symptoms you have been experiencing are simply those of a panic attack or relate to a post traumatic stress reaction then you will be able to deal with them with confidence.)

A panic attack (if we don't fuel it with more fear} will always peak and then begin to pass within minutes

Two main reasons for panic attacks

i Our security guard (amygdala) gets it wrong and makes a faulty pattern match to a danger.

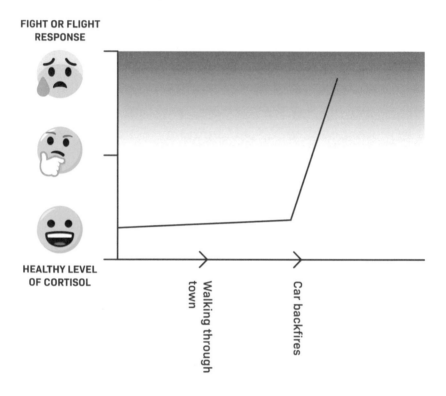

In this situation the amygdala has mistaken an innocent 'loud bang' for an extreme threat due to an earlier trauma.

ii Lots of little stressors build up in our lives (these can, of course include negative/distressing imaginings and thoughts).

Whether it is one huge leap that takes us to fight-or-flight, triggered by a loud bang, or several smaller steps as day-to-day stressors build up, the result, when we reach that crucial level, will be the same.

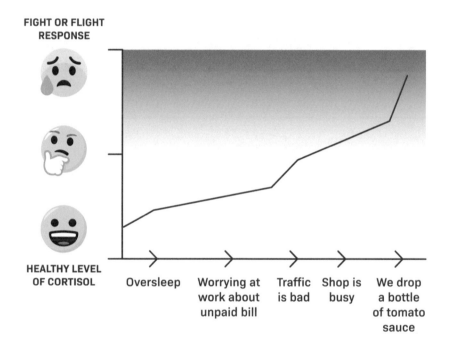

Our system, in simple terms, does not recognise what event it is that tips us over the edge. This is why, for some people, when background stress levels are already at a critical level, a smashed tomato ketchup, spilled orange juice, or a distressing thought can trigger a response that was originally designed for a life-threatening situation.

This response can be panic and fear <u>or</u> anger– but we'll continue to focus on the panic/fear first.

Starting the day stressed

It is important to understand too, that someone who has been traumatised will rarely (due to poor sleep and on-going difficulties in day-to-day life as a result of PTS) start a day off from a base-line of low stress.

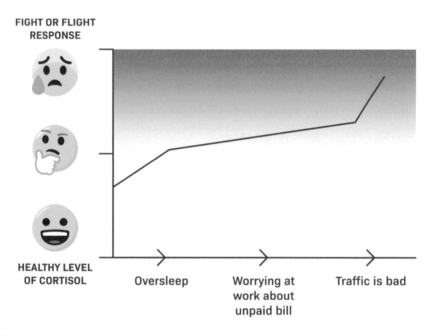

This means that a person beginning a day in this way might not even make it as far as the shop: the bad traffic is enough to tip them into a full fight-or-flight response. For some people, resilience is so low that simply waking up late (or receiving an unexpected bill in the morning post, or seeing a child spilling a glass of juice at breakfast) is all it takes.

It can feel as though your entire life is spent dipping in and out of states of extreme emotion.

Many of the men and women I've worked with over the years simply say, 'That's me – that's what it's like' when they look at this diagram.

Not an all-or-nothing state

"My thoughts start going round and round in circles. Sometimes I can't find the words I want. It sounds stupid but it's almost like I've forgotten how to speak." SG

It is important to recognise, too, that the fight-or-flight state is not an 'all' or 'nothing' state but, as you can see from the 'LIFE' diagrams, works on a sliding scale: the higher up the scale we rise, the more our body makes preparations for fighting or fleeing and the less access we have to our upper brain. This is why many people notice increased confusion, the inability to think straight, or to even find words to speak to be a warning sign of high levels of stress / anxiety – along with the physical symptoms of anxiety or rage, such as trembling, sweating, a pounding heart or digestive discomfort.

Understanding the symptoms of panic

It is important to recognise that all the terrifying and distressing symptoms of panic are simply the fight-or-flight response being fired at the wrong time.

• **Pounding heart** or palpitations: the heart pumps rapidly to circulate extra blood for running away or fighting.

• **Sweating**: the body is expecting to take vigorous exercise and needs to lose heat in order to avoid getting too hot.

• **Nausea or dry mouth**: digestion stops (as does production of saliva) so that extra blood can be diverted to the limbs.

• A sense of **needing to go to the loo**: again blood is diverted to the arms and legs and the kidneys/intestines stop working, causing the muscles controlling the anus and bladder to relax.

• **Rapid, shallow, breathing** (hyperventilation): more oxygen is taken on board to increase energy.

This increase in oxygen levels leads directly to several of the other symptoms of a panic attack:

• **Shortness of breath**: oxygen is a very sticky molecule and needs carbon dioxide to release it from the red blood cells which transport it around our system. When we breathe quickly we take in a lot of oxygen but exhale the carbon dioxide before it's had a chance to do its job so we feel oxygen-starved. The reality is that we have taken *too much* oxygen into our system.

• **Sharp chest pain**: caused by the strain on the chest muscles from hyperventilating.

- **Trembling and shaking**: this is a normal side-effect of hyperventilation – and the more hyperventilation, the worse it becomes.

- **Dizziness/numbness/weakness**: caused by hyperventilation and the resultant hypoxia (lack of oxygen to the brain).

- **Fear of losing control**: fight-or-flight has been fully turned on – even though there is nothing to fight or flee from. The overwhelming urge to escape from the narrow street lined with tall buildings is simply a reasonable reaction to what your security guard has mistakenly perceived as a real threat.

- Being **unable to think straight**, to remember words or to communicate: the thinking brain is being progressively shut down as the amygdala takes over

- A **sense of being unreal** (being in a dream or watching yourself going through a panic attack – which some people read as a sign that they are going mad) is simply a natural defence mechanism to try to calm down and prevent further distress.

- **Fear of dying**: without an understanding of why all these very real and distressing symptoms are occurring it is only natural that we would further fuel our fear with the belief that there must be something seriously and medically wrong.[v]

In a real life-or-death situation we would use this response up – the extra oxygen/blood circulated by our rapidly pumping heart – to fight or run away from danger. In the supermarket, when we've smashed the ketchup on the floor and this happens to be the tipping point at the end of a long day, or in the street when a car backfires and our jumpy security guard over-reacts, we instead experience the distressing symptoms as described above.

In Part 2 you will find specific techniques that can calm panic quickly and help alleviate these symptoms efficiently.

Understanding anger: the 'fight' response

"I'm always ready to flash ...sometimes the smallest things set me off and I just explode." DW

The other way the fight-or-flight response can go if fired at the wrong time is inappropriate anger. Many people notice fight-or-flight symptoms as a first sign that they are becoming angry:

• Trembling or shaking

• Heart pounding

• Breathing becoming more rapid and shallow

• Difficulty speaking

– or any of the other reactions detailed on the previous page.

Just as in a real survival situation, these symptoms are a sign that preparations are under way to make us as fast and strong as possible, and to allow our security guard to take charge and act in a split second – before rational thought has a chance to occur.

This can be a dangerous combination – especially if it occurs while driving our car, during arguments with our partner or if someone looks at us the wrong way.

When we are in this state we are literally 'not ourselves'– but the consequences of any actions our security guard takes when the boss is bound and gagged are ones that we will have to live with. When we get angry we 'use up' the physical preparations that our system has made and thus don't experience the terror of a panic attack – but it can be terrifying to others if our security guard regularly runs amok in response to a minor incident or false alarm.

It is really important to learn ways of calming down quickly if we know we are becoming angry in this way– if, say, a spilled juice or a sideways glance has the power to trigger this hugely powerful response.

In Part 2 you will find techniques you can use to calm down quickly in such situations, and avoid dangerous and damaging actions being taken by a primitive bit of your brain.

Understanding flashbacks

" I was on the bus with my boy heading into town and then, suddenly,
I was somewhere else – somewhere I didn't want to be. It was
embarrassing afterwards because my boy was really upset and people
were looking at me because they knew something was going on.
I still don't know what I was actually like when it happened.
I think they thought I was mad, or drunk, or something." MP

It often surprises people to learn that everyone has 'flashbacks'. For the majority of people who have not been badly traumatised, however, these are at a low level.

Many people have experienced, for example, a certain smell plunging them right back into a childhood memory, or hearing a song that strongly evokes emotions from their teenage years. How powerful the recall of such an event is simply depends on the strength of the emotional 'tag' attached to it.

If we have been through a trauma it is likely that the event will be tagged very powerfully, and encoded in the amygdala, which means that when something triggers a memory of it we can quite literally be taken right back there, re-experiencing vividly and horrifically the terrifying sights, sensations and smells of that time.

Why smells are so powerful

Of all our senses, smell is the only one that has a direct route to our security guard. All the others go via a part of the brain called the thalamus. This means that when we encounter a smell that reminds us of something (either pleasant or unpleasant) the effects are particularly powerful and instantaneous.

Understanding nightmares

"I always wake up sweating in the middle of the night. Last night I woke up screaming. I realised I was crouched down in the corner of the room and I'd peed the bed." SW

It is now increasingly widely recognised that when we dream we dream in metaphor. This means that we represent things that have happened to us during the day with things that are 'like' them from our internal memory store at night.[vi]

If we have experienced a trauma and it is 'on our mind' – or if we are reminded of it by many different things during the day – it is likely that the memories of this will be easily accessible. So, if we feel during the day that we . . .

• are 'trapped' in our daily life

• that someone is 'after' us (if only for the payment of a bill)

• that someone is injuring us or someone close to us

• that everyone is 'out to get us'

• that we can see 'no way out' of a situation

 . . . it is easy to see how these feelings can be represented by elements of a trauma memory at night – memories of being truly injured, trapped or chased, perhaps whilst on active service – resulting in a terrifying and vivid nightmare that recalls the original event or key elements of it.

Knock-on effects

"Everything is going out of control. I'm angry all the time – jumpy, snapping at the kids and missus. Some days I just can't get out of bed and get to work. I don't want to lose my family." MA

If our amygdala (security guard) is mistakenly pattern-matching to danger day and night so that we're constantly on the edge of fear or rage; if our daytime activities and night time rest are disturbed by flashbacks and nightmares; if our memory store is inaccessible due to high levels of stress chemicals; then it's no wonder that this has huge knock-on effects on the overall picture of our life.

We may:

• become jumpy and tense or angry, causing difficulties in our relationships with family, friends or colleagues.

• react violently or with terror to a particular trigger.

• feel incompetent or unable to do our job properly as we struggle to process or recall information.

• become increasingly exhausted and confused, struggling to take decisions.

• feel low or depressed.

• try to self-medicate to block out the pain with alcohol or drugs.

Without the right understanding, these difficulties can combine to make it feel as though life is gradually spiralling downhill and spinning out of control.

However, as the diagram on the next page and the explanation that follows show, rather than being random or separate difficulties, all of them are simply a natural result of the trauma experienced not yet having been processed.

With the right understanding and help, it is possible to begin finding ways of reversing this negative cycle, and beginning to set it turning in a more positive direction.

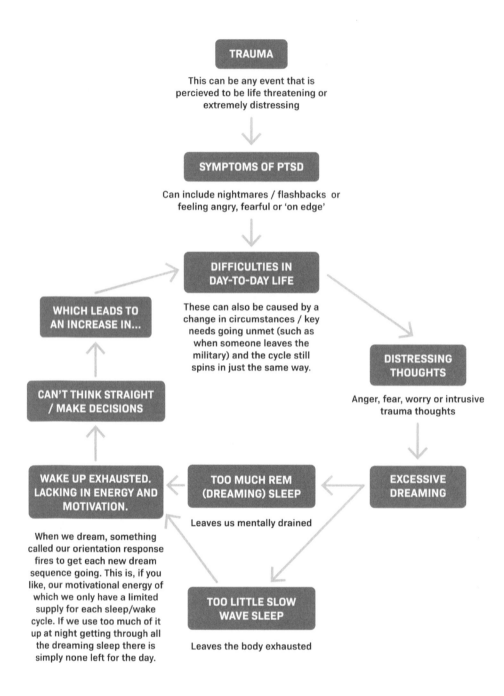

TRAUMA

This can be any event that is percieved to be life threatening or extremely distressing

SYMPTOMS OF PTSD

Can include nightmares / flashbacks or feeling angry, fearful or 'on edge'

DIFFICULTIES IN DAY-TO-DAY LIFE

These can also be caused by a change in circumstances / key needs going unmet (such as when someone leaves the military) and the cycle still spins in just the same way.

WHICH LEADS TO AN INCREASE IN...

DISTRESSING THOUGHTS

Anger, fear, worry or intrusive trauma thoughts

CAN'T THINK STRAIGHT / MAKE DECISIONS

WAKE UP EXHAUSTED. LACKING IN ENERGY AND MOTIVATION.

TOO MUCH REM (DREAMING) SLEEP

Leaves us mentally drained

EXCESSIVE DREAMING

When we dream, something called our orientation response fires to get each new dream sequence going. This is, if you like, our motivational energy of which we only have a limited supply for each sleep/wake cycle. If we use too much of it up at night getting through all the dreaming sleep there is simply none left for the day.

TOO LITTLE SLOW WAVE SLEEP

Leaves the body exhausted

How trauma can affect a whole life

"I wake up feeling more tired than when I went to bed. Every day
is a struggle to find the energy to do anything – even stuff
I used to really enjoy." MP

From the cycle on the facing page, it is clear why the remainder of the symptoms associated with PTS occur:

• Distressing thoughts during the day (anger and worry thoughts) relating to either the trauma or difficulties in daily life seriously disrupt the quality of our sleep. To discharge the emotional arousals that these create in our system we have long periods of intense and exhausting Rapid Eye Movement (REM) sleep, and thus have less time for Slow Wave Sleep (the sleep that repairs and restores our physical body).

• Low mood (depression), with its feelings of mental exhaustion and lack of motivation, is a natural result of this sleep disturbance and imbalance.

• Trying to escape from the pain and distress of this state by using alcohol and drugs, is not yet another illness (or co-morbidity, a term to strike terror into the heart of anyone) but a faulty coping strategy – and with help, better ones can be found.

The link between trauma, sleep and depression

" I go over and over stuff in my head – what's going to happen to me and the family if I don't get this sorted, and so many of the things that happened in Iraq or gone wrong in the past. It's like a broken record of worry and fear and anger just playing over and over again." SB

From the cycle illustrated on the previous page it is clear that anxiety, anger and trauma are closely linked to depression, and that disturbed sleep is an extremely common feature of depression. I have never yet had (and nor do I expect to) anyone who presents in my clinic with the symptoms of depression, or who has been diagnosed as being 'depressed', who has reported sleeping well and waking refreshed and full of energy each morning. Indeed, the ground-breaking work of psychologist Joe Griffin in this field has allowed an understanding of these 'mechanics' of depression to become a basis for helping people to break the cycle of low mood swiftly and effectively. [vii]

Sleep – especially the right amount of dreaming sleep – is essential to our emotional (and physical) health. We now know that the role of dreaming sleep is to deactivate emotional arousals that are not worked through to conclusion during waking hours. For example, if we bite our tongue rather than respond to a boss's cutting comment, the emotions aroused by this (unexpressed during waking hours) remain 'live'as an emotional arousal in our system and then have to be discharged through a dream. This frees up our brain, creating a clean slate, if you like, to face the next day's emotional concerns.

But 'worry' or 'anger' thoughts, often coupled in PTS with the sense of being constantly 'on guard' for terrors that never materialise and with repeatedly replaying distressing scenarios (all things that can never be dealt with or de-aroused in the present because they so often involve the past or future), mean that a person habitually thinking in this way will build up a huge stack of emotional arousals that need discharging through dreaming sleep at night. They completely overload the system. Having a few unexpressed arousals to work through in dreaming sleep is a system which works perfectly, and has evolved to allow us to function well. Having a whole cart-load causes huge problems.

Research in sleep laboratories has shown that depressed people have far more dreaming sleep than normal, to cope with this overload of unexpressed arousals. They begin dreaming earlier in the sleep cycle and then have more and more intense periods of REM sleep until the brain can take no more, and they wake exhausted in the early hours and begin worrying all over again.

This, combined with the fact that such a negatively active mind can make it hard to get off to sleep at all, means that they are simply not getting enough of the deep, slow-wave restorative sleep during which our body recovers – there simply isn't time! This can leave a sufferer not only physically exhausted, but also prone to picking up minor illnesses, or having flare-ups of immune related conditions such as asthma, arthritis or psoriasis.

On top of this – and the real killer in terms of mood – is that every time we begin to dream, something called our 'orientation response' fires. This is the response we need during waking hours to alert us to changes in our environment and to get us going on new tasks – our motivational energy if you like. When it fires at night, to tell us that there are un-discharged emotional arousals that need to be dealt with, it draws on our motivational energy, of which we only have a certain amount.

It is no wonder, then, that sufferers often wake in the morning feeling not just exhausted and easily upset, but lacking any motivation whatsoever to get them going. This understanding explains the complete mystery that exists for many of my patients when I start seeing them as to how they can sometimes have what seems to be a good night's sleep – quite a few hours with their eyes shut – but still wake up more tired than when they went to bed.

The truth is that when the balance between slow-wave sleep and dreaming sleep has been so wildly skewed, sleeping is indeed more tiring for the brain than being awake!

PART 2

Working towards recovery

Eight key steps to recovery

Based on the evidence so far, and with this understanding of PTS firmly in place, it is clear that there are several ways in which we can work within a holistic and scientifically based framework to bring about real and lasting positive change.

• **Process the traumatic memory** so that it no longer triggers distress.

• Begin to **recognise symptoms** for what they are and **learn to calm down swiftly** when they do arise.

• **Address any practical difficulties** that are contributing to raised stress levels, or seek help to do so – ensuring that all the elements we need as humans for a fulfilling life are in place.

• Learn to **lift low mood** and develop thinking skills to better **deal with the anger and worry thoughts** that contribute to the poor sleep that brings this about.

• Learn to prepare well to get **good sleep**.

• **Develop coping strategies** that alleviate suffering and do not (as the faulty ones of alcohol and drug use so often do) simply create more.

• Build a healthy lifestyle that supports recovery, including **physical exercise** and **improvements in diet**.

• Find out where to **seek effective support** in doing some or all of the above

*The next pages will outline starting points for these **eight key steps to recovery** . . .*

Step 1
Processing a traumatic memory

As we established at the start, we have the natural process for dealing with threats hard-wired in us, and as one would expect for something that had survived the 'weeding out' of evolutionary change, the natural process for calming down. In PTS something blocks this calming down from happening and thus, to return to our old friend common sense, anything that is going to work to aid recovery must aid and support this natural process.

Dealing with a trauma memory centres on allowing the system to calm down enough for the hippocampus (filing cabinet) to begin communicating with the amygdala (security guard) about it. We need our rational brain to get a look at the memory so that it can add some details and file it more accurately as something that happened at a specific time, in a specific place, in a specific set of circumstances in the past. It is not about 'taking away' the memory of something that has happened in the past – however distressing – but about allowing it to be stored in a way that is part of our narrative history, not as an active 'danger' alert, with red flags waving and alarms being sounded each time it is recalled.

Talking

For many people, talking is an important part of calming down and processing the traumatic memory.

As we discuss what happened, trying to explain events so that another will understand, or listening to another person's 'take' on what occurred, our rational brain begins to engage with the memory and we are on the road to processing it effectively

It will probably always be a strong memory, perhaps painful or unpleasant, but it will cease to be a simplistic template for danger on 'red-alert' triggering the fight-or-flight response.

When to talk and who to talk to

Choosing someone to talk to who we trust and who we feel understands where we are coming from (not necessarily a trained counsellor) is key. If we speak to someone who we feel doesn't understand (which may well make us feel angry or upset), then we are simply adding another stressor into our system while trying to engage with the memory – which, of course, makes the security guard far more likely to remain in charge of it.

If we notice that we begin to feel better after talking about the event with a sympathetic person, then that is a sure sign that this processing is happening effectively.

When to seek other help

For some people, however, especially those with a vivid imagination, any attempt to recall the memory or discuss the event – even with someone with whom they feel entirely comfortable, or with a counsellor – leads them to re-engage with it so completely that they re-experience it and thus run the risk of re-traumatising themselves. (The brain, in simple terms, cannot distinguish between a strongly imagined event and a real one.)

If you experience extreme distress that deepens each time you recall the trauma, or if you are undergoing counselling which requires you to repeatedly revisit or talk about the trauma and you find that this is increasing your distress, this is a sign that you should perhaps seek more specialist help.

Finding a therapist who has been specifically trained in the treatment of trauma is essential.

As with any specialist skill we have to 'buy in' during our lifetime, be it washing-machine repair, house re-plastering or surgical attention, we must find evidence that the person we are entrusting with the task has a good track record of competence in that specific field. However, while it is relatively easy to check out the water-tightness of a neighbour's chimney, or even to ask about the track record of a particular heart consultant, in the world of mental health it is sometimes somewhat harder to ascertain the same information about a therapist and their outcomes. There are many good therapists out there who *do* have the specific understanding and skills necessary to work effectively with trauma, but finding them can be a little more tricky. Asking some questions before engaging in lengthy (and often expensive) therapy can be essential. Key questions to ask might include:

• What experience they have in working with PTSD.

• What outcomes have they helped clients achieve.

• Whether therapy will involve 'just talking' or whether they will be working in a targeted and specific way with the trauma memory and any attendant symptoms, such as depression or anxiety.

> *"I can talk about the things that happened now. Things that I thought I'd never be able to. They still upset me, but not the same way any more." AJ*

Step 2
Dealing with symptoms effectively

Alongside working to process the trauma memory itself, it is also essential to learn ways of making it less likely that unpleasant symptoms will arise – and, if they do, to be able to recognise them for what they are as swiftly as possible. As will now be clear, *all* symptoms of PTS occur because the levels of stress chemicals in our system are inappropriately high.

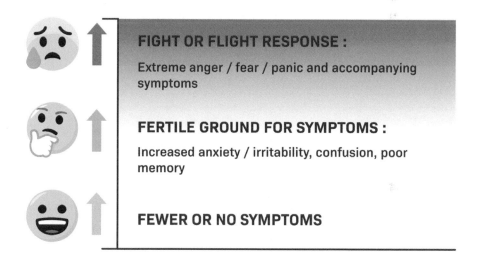

FIGHT OR FLIGHT RESPONSE :

Extreme anger / fear / panic and accompanying symptoms

FERTILE GROUND FOR SYMPTOMS :

Increased anxiety / irritability, confusion, poor memory

FEWER OR NO SYMPTOMS

Anything we do needs to be about:

• 'Switching off' flight-or-flight if it is on the way to being fired inappropriately

   or

• 'Mopping it up', if it has been fired, as swiftly and effectively as possible.

Anything we do to **calm our system down** lessens the intensity of symptoms associated with PTS.

> *"I know now I've got some things I can do to prevent things getting bad or to change the way I'm feeling if something does set me off. Remembering to do the right stuff is sometimes hard but I know it works and I feel like I'm getting there."* MW

i Learning to 'calm down'

"Doing the gym and getting out running is what it's all about for me. It's how I keep things under control and let off steam. When I don't do them – that's when stuff starts going wrong." MH

Relaxing and calming down is not necessarily about sitting in a chair doing nothing. It is anything, any activity we undertake, that allows the level of stress chemicals in our system to drop.

We can calm down in a number of ways, including by taking vigorous physical activity. Here are some of the ones that the clients I work with find most useful.

Vigorous physical activities

Many of the difficulties associated with PTS occur because the fight-or-flight response spends a lot of time 'all dressed up with no-where to go'. Fight-or-flight is all about our system getting ready to take vigorous physical activity. Simply put, if we take vigorous physical activity, we use it up.

Such activities might include:

Running
Cycling
Climbing
Surfing
Walking
Going to the gym
Swimming
Riding

Pleasurable/distraction activities

If we focus on the unpleasant feelings or sensations experienced when stress levels are high it tends to increase our awareness of them and make us feel increasingly distressed. If we can focus away from them onto other things, they tend to naturally lessen.

Such activities might include:

Reading a book
Listening to the radio
Meeting with a friend
Watching a film
Gardening
Any of the physical activities listed on the previous page

For many people, undertaking some form of work (paid or voluntary, formal or informal) can act in this way too. Many people find that hours alone in an empty house with little to do leads to an increase in negative thoughts and thus also to an increase in the symptoms they experience.

"Making models is that time for me. I just focus on what I'm doing and it stops my mind spinning. I use it as a reward to get me motivated to do other stuff too." IF

ii Self-help tool: 7/11 breathing

> *" I can't believe something so simple can help so much.*
> *It's just like an 'off' switch when I'm losing it." MP*

I always start with an apology when I introduce this breathing technique in a therapy session.

Often I am sitting with someone whose life is in pieces. They have possibly lost their career, marriage and children to the symptoms they are struggling with – have possibly even tried to take their own life – and then here is some silly woman sitting opposite them telling them that breathing differently will help. It almost seems disrespectful to the magnitude of their suffering to suggest such a seemingly insignificant technique.

The scientific reality, however, is that this simple breathing technique is one of the most powerful tools that any of us can have at our disposal because it works directly with our system to switch off fight-or-flight. It allows the rational brain to stay in charge and any symptoms to lessen as the stress levels fall.

The steps are:

• Breathe in for a count of 7

• Breathe out for a count of 11 (both through your nose, if possible).

Make sure that when you are breathing in, you are doing 'diaphragmatic breathing' (your tummy rises and falls as you breathe) rather than shallower upper chest breathing. If you find that it's difficult to lengthen your breaths to a count of 7 and 11, then reduce the count to breathing in to 3 and out to 5, or whatever suits you best, as long as the out-breath is longer than the in-breath.

Many of the veterans that I work with have been chronically over-breathing for years in correspondence with the stress that they have been under for a prolonged period of time. For some of them extending the out-breath can feel very uncomfortable to begin with as they are so used to functioning in a different mode. What I suggest in such cases is that they simply begin by re-balancing that breathing to, say, 3 in and 3 out, and then gradually extend the out-breath when they are comfortable with that.

This technique is so powerful because it works directly with our physiological system. Our out-breath stimulates what is called the parasympathetic nervous system, a natural bodily response that enables us to 'rest-and-digest' – the very opposite of 'fight-or-flight'. Out-breaths decrease blood pressure, slow the heart rate and rebalance oxygen levels in your system, lowering emotional arousal in the process.

The clients I work with are advised to use this technique in two ways:

• To take it as you would a medication, at least three times a day for 5–10 minutes (it doesn't matter whether it's before or after mealtimes!) as a guaranteed way of lowering levels of stress and emotional arousal. The more you practice, the more apparent its effects will become, and this practice will also stand you in good stead for when you need to use it.

• As a rescue measure. If you notice feelings of fear, panic or anger beginning to rise, simply breathe out. Focus on lengthening the out breath and making the in breath less important, going into a few minutes of the counted breathing to allow your system to calm down and your rational brain to regain control.

iii Self Help Tool: Becoming AWARE of how to beat panic

This simple technique has been used by many people to limit the distress caused by a panic attack and gradually to reduce the number they experience.

Accept

Accept the fact that your system is so overloaded that it has fired the fight-or-flight response inappropriately. Remind yourself that this is a normal and natural response; that the feelings you have, whilst undoubtedly unpleasant, are not dangerous and that they will pass soon enough.

Watch

Try to take a step back from the experience and watch the panic as an observer. Notice what symptoms you have and perhaps scale them each for severity on a scale of one to ten.

Act normally

Try to continue with whatever you are doing. Breathe normally with focus on making the out-breath longer, or use 7/11 breathing (*see page 57*).

Repeat

Continue to accept the symptoms of fight-or-flight;watch them; scale them; and act normally until the panic attack goes down to a comfortable level.

Expect the best

Expect and remind yourself that the symptoms you are currently experiencing will pass and that each time you successfully handle a panic attack in this way you make it less likely that you will experience one again, and more likely that you will be able to calm down effectively and quickly if you do.

iv Self-help tool: Calming down when anger flashes

Anger is one of the essential tools we humans have for our survival. If we are in real danger, it is anger and the firing of the fight-or-flight response that might well save our life. But when it is being fired inappropriately – with huge explosions resulting from small incidents – it can make us a danger to ourselves and others.

When we are very angry our security guard is beginning to take control of our brain and this means that, as we established earlier, we can take actions before conscious awareness and thought. We can find that we have punched someone, rammed a car or slapped our partner *before* we are consciously aware of what we are doing. For this reason it is key to learn ways of recognising the very first signs of anger and doing something that ensures we do not become a danger to ourselves or others.

Get good at noticing the physical / mental signs that anger is mounting.

You may only have seconds to do this before the security guard completely takes over – so you need to become very good at it. Does your heart rate quicken? Do you notice yourself becoming 'hot under the collar' and sweating? Do you notice yourself trembling with rage?

For some people, the signs are mental: as their upper brain, and the bits that deal with language, become inaccessible, they either feel a fog or red mist descending, or they find it difficult to find words to speak.

Take steps to calm or move away from this anger

There are many ways to do this. Some people find a calming breathing technique such as 7/11 very useful and can use it to calm down *in situ*. Others find that something that forces the boss to engage, such as counting backwards in threes from 50 (a task that the security guard simply cannot perform), is enough to keep their rational, thinking brain in control. For some, however – especially those who experience a 'vertical take-off' when it comes to anger – simply getting out of the situation as quickly as possible is necessary.

Physical exercise is an excellent accompaniment to this: if you go for a run, cycle or brisk walk it uses up some of the chemicals associated with stress that are flooding your system.

It is important to remember, however, that it takes at least twenty minutes for an anger response to 'wash through' your system. If you return to a situation sooner than that, or you spend part of that time out going over just how angry you are, you may feel calmer but, in reality, you are primed to explode at the slightest trigger.

"I was actually really scared I was going to kill someone. It happened so quickly – me going from calm to wanting to just punch their face in. Now I try to recognise the signs and do something straight away to calm down or get out of the situation. I didn't want to end up really hurting someone." SG

v Building Resilience

In the early part of the book, we focused on how various events in our lives (unexpected bills, bad traffic, difficulties at work) can push us up closer and closer to the point at which fight-or-flight is programmed to kick in.

What is really important to understand now is that the self-help tools on the previous pages do exactly the opposite. These take us away from fight-or-flight and can become an important resource for us to draw on in our day-to-day life. It can be easy to dismiss things like getting out in the garden, going for a walk, watching a good film, or doing some photography as not 'serious' or 'medical' enough to deal with the very real physical and emotional symptoms of distress being experienced.

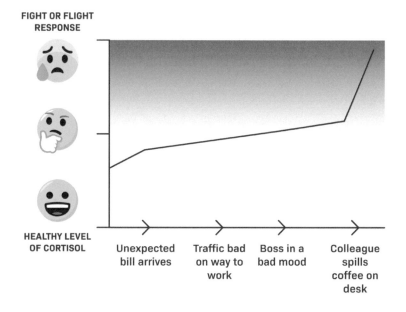

Surely such huge and serious problems must require a huge and dramatic intervention? Heavy medication at the very least? But just compare the LIFE diagram at the bottom of the previous page with the one on this page: one person trying to simply struggle on through difficulties, the other using such resources to counter the effects of these difficulties.

By mid-morning the person on the previous page is experiencing the extreme rage or terror of fight-or-flight being inappropriately triggered by a minor incident. And not only do they have to deal with this immediate level of distress but later on, when they have calmed down, they will probably also have to pick up the pieces and apologise for the choice words their 'security guard' had with that colleague about clumsiness and coffee cups . . .

With resource activities built in, however, even with an equally high 'background' level of stress, the second person manages the same day far more successfully.

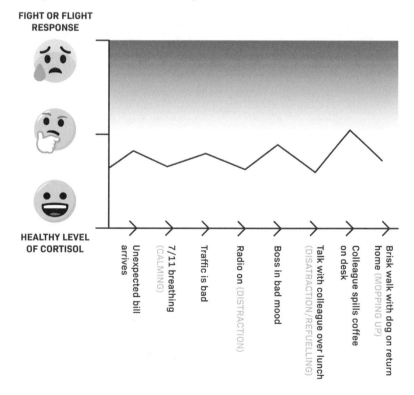

Exercise:
Spend a few moments making a list of the activities that could become your resource activities, deployed intelligently to improve your own experience of each day.

From experience, I would suggest that alongside the things that you already do (or used to do but have stopped for some reason – perhaps lack of motivation) 7/11 breathing should always be included and practised, as it is something that can be used at any time and in any setting where there is need to calm the symptoms you are experiencing and get the 'the boss' back in charge.

Keep the list somewhere to hand so that you have it to refer to if things are getting tough because, when stress levels rise, the rational brain (the bit that stores information about coping tools, strategies and resource activities) is out of action and you can guarantee that your security guard won't remember them or remind you to use them!

"Since getting help I can see these patterns in my life. I have a picture of one of those LIFE charts in my mind and I'm better now at knowing when stressors are building up and when I need to do stuff to stop things getting out of control." AJ

vi Dealing with flashbacks and nightmares

As we have seen, both flashbacks and nightmares occur when a primitive bit of our brain misjudges things, and it feels as if events that happened in the past are actually happening right now, in the present. Working with this knowledge it is clear that anything that will help us to deal with nightmares and flashbacks will

• work quickly to calm our system down and put the rational brain back in control

• begin to draw out the differences (rather than any partial similarities) between the past trauma and the present set of circumstances.

I have already outlined some tools that you can use to effectively calm down – such as 7/11 breathing – but combining this with the reassurance of the following two exercises can be a powerful way of lowering the levels of distress experienced and, gradually, lessening the number or intensity of nightmares/flashbacks experienced.

vii Self-help tool: That was then . . . this is now

As discussed, the fight-or-flight response, when fired repeatedly in PTS, is all about the security guard (amygdala) getting it wrong, and thinking that a danger or distress that occurred in the past is recurring every time it makes a match to any part of that 'pattern' in the present.

Beginning to give feedback to your system that the event(s) that traumatised you are firmly in the past is a way that many clients I have worked with have found useful to begin to move on from the memory.

That was then . . . this is now is a powerful technique for arresting a trigger (a faulty pattern match made by the security guard) in its tracks – and can stop flashbacks occurring or lessen their severity.

The secret is to practise saying

'That was then . . . this is *now*'

on a regular basis, so that it's ready to use in an instant. It is important to slow down your speech, lower the tone of your voice and say the sentence forcefully, with the emphasis on a long 'noowww!' This lengthy final word also extends the out breath and taps into the principle behind the breathing technique that you have already learned.

This technique, and many others which help in similar ways, can be found in the excellent book *Beating Combat Stress: 101 Techniques for Recovery.*[ix]

viii Self-help tool: Dual awareness

The following script has helped many people affected by trauma to begin to deal effectively with those times when they feel that they are re-living the event. In the areas marked with an asterisk, insert and use words that reflect your own situation. Speak slowly, making each statement deliberate and important.

There seem to be two things going on here.

I am feeling *scared/angry/on edge/isolated** because something has triggered a strong memory of the *bomb blast/RTA/ambush.**

My body feels *tense/shaky/like my heart is going to jump out of my chest.**

But at the same time, I know that this incident happened some time ago and I am also aware that right now I am here, in this *room/place** and I know that because I can see . . .

(List five things you can see: for example *the picture on the wall, my bed in the corner, the flowers on the patio decking)**

I can hear . . .

(List three things you can hear: *the birds singing in the trees, the sound of the breeze, the traffic on the road)**

I can sense . . .

List three things you can sense: *the warmth of the sun on my face, the softness of the sand under my feet, the sheets of my bed on my skin)**

Because of these things I know that (*the bomb blast/RTA/ambush**) is not happening now. [x]

ix Putting 'You' back in control

"Ros said to me to try this and I thought she'd gone nuts. But it worked. I'm not having him wreck things for me anymore." MP

Before we conclude this section it would be remiss of me not to make one final reference to our friend the security guard.

The bottom line is that he causes utter chaos in so many lives, getting stuff wrong, jumping up and down in rage or running off in a panic, taking action on our behalf and then leaving our rational brain – our true self – to pick up the pieces once he has calmed down.

How many times have you thought afterwards, 'Why did I react like that?' How many times has he caused you to snap at someone you care about – or forced you to leave or avoid a venue that you once would have visited with ease or enjoyment?

He is an exquisitely stupid bit of the brain when put in charge of the wrong areas of our life (that is, any that don't involve *real* life-or-death situations) and the sooner we are able to separate ourselves from his thoughts and actions the sooner we place our boss firmly back in control.

It may sound silly, but from years of experience in working with traumatised and distressed clients, one of the things that many of them find incredibly useful is to give this pesky individual a name and identity that separates his input from that of our rational brain.

For example, one of the clients I am working with at the moment has named his 'Jonesey' after the character Corporal Jones in Dad's Army – always running around panicking or shouting. Another, whose security guard has taken him to see very dark places in the past, damaging both himself and others around him in the process, has named his 'the Hulk'.

And there is method in this seeming madness. The only bit of the brain that is intelligent enough, and has the capacity, to step back and notice that a thought is not rational, *is* our rational brain. By labelling and naming our fear and anger and other emotionally charged thoughts as belonging to the security guard, we are forcing our rational brain to stay in charge and thus correspondingly keeping the boss in charge and our brain and physiology in a calmer state.

This technique will not magically or entirely shut him up. But it will, within the context of the other suggestions in this book, work with what is going on to begin to take the edge off things. Be quite forceful with him if necessary. If he starts getting involved, tell him in any language that feels appropriate to sling his hook and stop bothering you. Make him a comedy figure of fun, an ineffectual and ridiculous monster, a really stupid and brainless oaf that to date has been getting involved in stuff way above his pay grade.

Begin to put him back in the box where he belongs: you may be surprised by the results . . .

Step 3
Getting our needs met

i The elements of a fulfilling life

One of the things I often do early on in our work together, when seeking to understand how I can best support a traumatised veteran, civilian or family member, is ask them to complete a Wheel of Life. This is a tool based on the latest understanding of the needs we all share as human beings and which must be met in order for us to enjoy emotionally healthy lives.[xi] It identifies which areas of someone's life are working well and which areas of their life are currently adding to their stress.

If someone had suffered a trauma to their knee, perhaps been in-volved in a nasty accident, they would undoubtedly be referred to a physical specialist – someone who understood how to help mend shattered knees and who would be able to oversee any rehabilitative work that needed to be carried out. But the key thing is this: in order to be able to do any of that work effectively, that physical specialist would have to have a good understanding of what a healthy, fully functioning knee looked like. They would then have something to work back towards.

The same truth applies when dealing with a life that has suffered a trauma. Anyone involved in its repair and rehabilitation, whether the patient themselves or a clinical professional should have a good understanding of what a healthy, fully functioning life looks like and how it works. Without that we are all working in the dark, without any clear idea of where we are aiming to get to.

ii Self-help tool: The Wheel of Life

Spend a few moments filling in the Wheel of Life on the next page for yourself. Indicate with a cross in each section how well you feel that area of your life is functioning at the moment – and remember, this tool is not just a snapshot of how things are at the moment but is also always a map for positive change.

Many of the clients that I work with start off with the majority of their scores in the dark blue area, but gradually things begin to improve as first one then another area begins to be addressed and come right.

When you have completed yours, begin to see whether there are any areas that you can see *any* possibility of improving – perhaps spending a little more time doing something you enjoy, eating healthily or getting out for some exercise.

Positive change is a little like rolling a snowball downhill; to begin with we have to push it ourselves but, as its size increases, its own momentum takes over.

Whatever your wheel looks like at the moment, the understanding it contains can be the start of a plan for positive change (if change is needed) or for informed maintenance if all is going well.

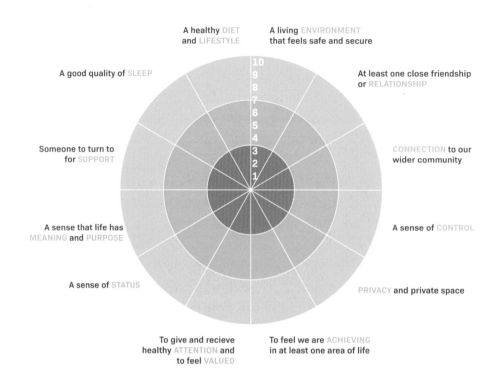

A healthy DIET and LIFESTYLE

A living ENVIRONMENT that feels safe and secure

A good quality of SLEEP

At least one close friendship or RELATIONSHIP

Someone to turn to for SUPPORT

CONNECTION to our wider community

A sense that life has MEANING and PURPOSE

A sense of CONTROL

A sense of STATUS

PRIVACY and private space

To give and recieve healthy ATTENTION and to feel VALUED

To feel we are ACHIEVING in at least one area of life

A detailed explanation of areas covered by the Wheel of Life:

A secure **ENVIRONMENT**: a physically and mentally secure environment. We don't have to live in a grand house, but we do need a place that meets our physical needs for shelter and warmth – somewhere we don't feel bullied or under threat, physically or emotionally.

A close **RELATIONSHIP**: someone who totally accepts and understands us and who we can turn to for SUPPORT.

CONNECTION to our **COMMUNITY**: we are designed as human beings to belong to a tribe or group and our brain does not function as well in isolation. When we are isolated, our thinking tends to become more distressed and distressing.

CONTROL: the feeling that we are an active agent in our life – that we have the power to change things through the decisions we make and the actions we take, rather than life just happening to us.

PRIVACY: a place where we can escape from the demands of life and have time to reflect. As with all needs, there has to be a balance, though, as too much privacy can become isolation.

ACHIEVEMENT: this sense can come from work/a hobby/ a particular role we fulfil.

ATTENTION: to feel that people notice us for the right reasons and that we notice others and that we are valued for what we do.

STATUS: a sense of what our position is in the world – of who we are, what we do and how the world sees us.

MEANING and **PURPOSE**: the thing that keeps us going when things get really tough. This could be a role that we fill, a belief system or dedication to a particular area of life.

SUPPORT: this could come from our close relationship or community, but might be someone we turn to as a professional.

SLEEP: a good quality of sleep is essential. The number of hours is not set in stone – if we are awakening feeling refreshed and ready for the day then we are getting the right amount.

HEALTHY DIET and **LIFESTYLE**: the right kinds of fuel and maintenance (including exercise, hobbies and fun) are essential for us both physically and emotionally. Things that reliably make us feel good are not luxuries at the end of a long 'to do' list, but the essential building blocks of an emotionally healthy life.

iii Addressing practical difficulties that increase our stress

Dealing effectively with any practical difficulties relating to our day-to-day situation is, then, a key part of moving on from the effects of trauma. Trauma, and the ripple effect that it creates through our lives if untreated for many years (relationship breakdown, difficulties at work, debt, alcohol misuse, to name but a few), can become a self-perpetuating spiral of decline which, in turn, continually puts a sufferer's system closer to that point at which symptoms of distress are likely to be experienced.

These practical difficulties can be a very real block to an individual beginning to get more of their needs met effectively. Working to address these difficulties enables them to move away from the high levels of stress that result from needs not being met and which, in turn, allow symptoms of PTS to flourish.

Helping clients to seek appropriate support to alleviate such difficulties is a key part of helping them to move forward, and thus should be a key part of any good therapist's role. Often a good GP or the Citizens Advice Bureau (CAB) can offer advice as to local or national organisations that can help in dealing with difficulties such as debt, isolation or housing. For veterans of the armed forces, the Royal British Legion (RBL) and Soldiers, Sailors, Airmen and Families Association (SSAFA), as well as service-specific and local support charities, can be good at signposting.

If you are aware that such practical difficulties exist in your life, and you know that they are raising the stress levels of everyday living, then even seeking support to get one small part of what at times can seem an overwhelming picture sorted can be a huge step forward. It often not only stops some of the negative ripple effect but also sets up a positive one all of its own.

If, for example, you are able to consolidate a debt or work out a repayment plan, not only is a huge pressure taken off in that particular area of your life but it could be that it leaves you a little extra financial room for something you enjoy – perhaps for visits to a gym or swimming pool. And as well as the physical benefits of doing such activities, those visits could result in a friendship made in that setting gradually developing . . . You see how it works.

iv Addressing difficulties in adjusting to civilian life

> *"It felt like I'd lost everything when I left – my friends, my job,*
> *all the stuff I enjoyed doing and believed in."* MW

An understanding of the needs we all share as human beings, contained in the Wheel of Life, combined with the understanding of the symptoms we experience when we come under stress and move towards the state of fight-or-flight, explains the distress some military personnel experience on leaving the military – and which is sometimes diagnosed, rather frighteningly, as 'Adjustment Disorder'.

On leaving the military (or indeed any role that a person has put their all into), they will often leave behind at the very least:

• Their career, which gave them a sense of status and competence

• The community to which they were connected, and within which they may have developed hobbies and socialised

• Close friendships

• A structured and healthy lifestyle

• The institution and the service to their country which may have given their life 'purpose and meaning'

When we imagine what happens to the picture of someone's life (as captured on the Wheel of Life) after so many needs are knocked out in one go, it is clear why they come under extreme stress.

The symptoms of 'Adjustment Disorder'

The symptoms for 'Adjustment Disorder' (as listed in the official DSM diagnostic manual) can include:

• **Psychological symptoms**: These include anxiety, worry, poor concentration and irritability and depression.

• **Physical symptoms**: These include palpitations, rapid breathing, diarrhoea and tremor.

• **Behavioural disturbances**: These can consist of aggression, abuse of alcohol, drug misuse, social difficulties, and occupational problems.

It is no coincidence that these symptoms (sometimes seen as those of yet another separate 'illness') are simply the symptoms of fight-or-flight and, just as in PTS, the knock-on effects of this. With so many needs suddenly unmet, our stress levels rise and our primitive amygdala judges that it must be under some threat. The move towards the state where it can effectively run from, or do combat with, a danger begins.

For a reminder of the symptoms of fight-or-flight, and to compare them to the symptoms of adjustment disorder, turn back to page 34. It can also be useful to revisit the cycle illustrated on page 42 and see how leaving the military can cause increased difficulties in day to day life, which leads in turn to increased worry or anger thoughts, to poor sleep, and on to feelings of low mood and possibly the use of faulty coping strategies.

Can PTS be brought on by leaving the military?

Many people do not immediately experience symptoms relating to a traumatic incident. Sometimes these emerge many years later (usually during or after a period of increased stress), and many of the veterans that I work with report that they first experienced nightmares or flashbacks about traumas which had occurred years earlier only on leaving the military.

If we recognise that . . .

• leaving the military can lead to many basic, emotional needs going unmet

• when these needs go unmet our background stress levels rise

. . . it is clear why leaving the military can leave individuals operating in a zone where fertile conditions for symptoms exist.

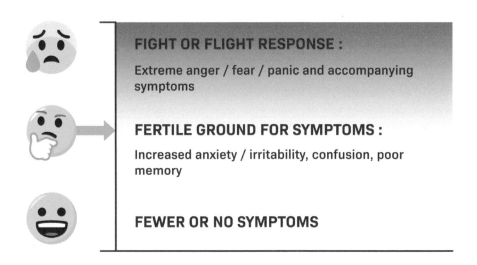

FIGHT OR FLIGHT RESPONSE :

Extreme anger / fear / panic and accompanying symptoms

FERTILE GROUND FOR SYMPTOMS :

Increased anxiety / irritability, confusion, poor memory

FEWER OR NO SYMPTOMS

Step 4
Lifting low mood

*"I was waking up in a fog every morning. Some days
I couldn't even be bothered to wash or get dressed." JC*

i Living with depression

Low mood (often diagnosed in clinical terms as depression), is something that, if present, can really stand in the way of recovery. It not only makes us feel awful – its symptoms being characterised by a loss of energy and motivation (as described in the cycle on page 42) – but these symptoms themselves then stand in the way of us having the wherewithal to do the things we need to do to get it to lift.

It lies to us about the pointlessness and hopelessness of everything, tells us that we should stay in bed or indoors rather than engaging with life, and instructs us that nothing will ever get better. It sucks the joy and sense of being truly 'alive' out of life. It can also take some sufferers, via these thought processes, to some very dark places indeed, where life itself seems hardly worth continuing with.

If this is the case for you (if you have been or are experiencing suicidal thoughts or feelings), then it is essential to get good professional help, perhaps starting with your GP or contacting one of the crisis organisations available to both veterans and civilians. Obviously, the subject of depression is one which deserves an entire guide to itself, and an excellent one which has helped many of those who suffer has already been written: *How to Lift Depression . . . Fast,* by Joe Griffin and Ivan Tyrrell.[xii]

I cannot recommend this book highly enough or stress how many people, veterans and civilians, have been helped by the information it contains. Depression, as this guide makes clear, is simply an added layer of suffering in an already difficult life – and one which can be swiftly lifted when we understand enough to do so.

And there are many things that we can do as individuals to break the cycle of low mood illustrated on those earlier pages – things we can begin to do right away and that will have rapid results. The preceding sections of this second part of the guide have already illustrated key elements of the process that will allow you to face each day, whatever difficulties and challenges it may bring, with at least a little hope and determination – both of which are key to any kind of recovery from any kind of difficulty, and both of which low mood/depression so effectively steals. I am sure that even if things are very difficult right now, you may well be able to recall a time, before depression set in, when you would have faced a difficult day with a measure of energy and hope, rather than it all simply feeling too much.

ii Dealing effectively with distressing and emotionally arousing thoughts

"My mind just never seemed to stop and most of it was really negative stuff. Now I notice if I start thinking that way, and I do something to stop it because I know it just drags me down otherwise." AJ

Thoughts that create strong negative emotions in us (be they anger, fear, worry, shame, guilt or blame) are damaging. They disrupt our day, leaving our decisions and actions increasingly in the hands of our security guard – which can, and regularly does, lead to chaos and yet further distress. They also, and equally damagingly, stop us from getting off to sleep and then disrupt the quality and balance of that rest, leaving us in danger of waking feeling low and exhausted. Such thinking, as the cycle on page 42 shows, is the driving force for generating depression.

If you are someone who has been thinking this way quite a lot recently – or perhaps have always thought this way – the idea of being able to stop doing so might seem impossible. I know it certainly did to me, many years ago, when I began to recognise that worrying, far from simply being a distressing pastime which I seemed to have got rather good at, was actually in danger of making me quite unwell.

Simply telling someone to stop worrying or stop over-thinking things, however, is (as I also know from experience) as much use as putting up a chocolate fire-guard. But if we begin to think of these particular ways of thinking as a skill – and not a good one at that, but one which we have been practising and practising for years until we are now an expert – then that leaves room, as in any other area of life, for us to learn a new skill, a better way of doing it.

To begin with, however, as with any new way of doing something as we try for better results – be that learning a new way to hold a tennis racket, a different hand position while playing a musical instrument, a new procedure for a task at work – it will feel difficult, alien, unnatural or impossible ever to master. But with practice, all of those things improve to the point where the old way of doing it is largely forgotten and the new way becomes our 'default' setting for whatever activity it may be. It is no different with the skills that we practise in terms of thinking.

Not responding with churning and repetitive worry, anger, frustration or fear *will* at first feel alien, impossible and as if it could never change. But with concrete new techniques in place, it is very possible to make this new thinking skill one over which you have mastery – with the very real prize being a good night of balanced sleep, and freedom from the dragging, exhausting weight of unmanaged depression.

iii Self-help tool: Dealing with worry thoughts

"I didn't believe I could ever stop them. From the moment I woke up in the morning – or the middle of the night – and then on and on. Never getting anywhere. But I did. It worked." LW

Understanding and taking the following steps can play a key part in ensuring that worries cease to get in the way of your life, and stop setting in motion a chain of knock-on effects that leave you feeling exhausted and lacking in motivation.

1 **Get good at identifying worry thoughts as soon as they arise**.

Stick a label on them in your mind. I often say to the veterans that I work with: 'If you can spot the enemy on a far ridge and use long-range weapons to deal with them, it is far better than just letting them advance and advance until you end up locked in a bloody hand-to-hand combat from which it is far harder to emerge unscathed.' Spot worry thoughts in the distance, clearly identify them for the enemy that they are, and then deal with them effectively and firmly.

2 Ask yourself one key question each time you do notice one: **'Can I do anything practical to sort this out now?'**

3 If the answer is **'YES'** – such as check that you taxed the car, or write the letter to the council that has been hanging over you – then **do it now**, or make a concrete plan to do it.

If the answer is **'NO'**, use one of the following strategies to get rid of it and **set it aside**, reminding yourself that the only thing it will do is disrupt your sleep if you continue with it.

I often ask a client when they are going over and over the same difficulty that is troubling them: 'If I let you have my room and that comfy chair you're in for the whole of the rest of the day, and told you to think about this subject for the rest of the day, do you think you would come to a conclusion regarding it?' The answer, invariably, is 'No'. The sooner we realise that the *only* thing that worrying will ever achieve is too much dreaming sleep, not enough slow wave sleep and feelings of depression, then the sooner we can begin to set it aside with real determination.

Put worry on hold
Write your worry thought down and keep it to look at afresh the next day or to discuss with someone who supports you.

Distract yourself
If you try to simply 'stop worrying' or 'stop feeling angry' you end up with a hole in your life. Your mind has got used to feasting on a lot of worry/anger/fear. If someone who was trying to give up eating cake simply cleared all the cake from their house leaving empty shelves and cupboards, they would be likely to miss it hugely and be off to the shops to get more. If, however, they had made sure that those places where the cake used to be were filled with other, better things to eat, they would be more likely to succeed. Make sure you have something in place for your mind to gets its teeth into.

Perhaps turn to one of your resource activities instead. (*Look back to page 64 for a reminder of what these were.*) Another huge success that many of my clients have had is in using story CDs or an online app like Audible to make sure that if their mind needs distraction there is always something of interest with which to feed it. Unlike a book (as the concentration required for reading is often hard for PTS sufferers, and it requires sitting down and using your hands) a story or pod-cast on a phone can be playing while you get on with your day.

Spend less time alone

Being alone with your thoughts can be a stressful place to be if your thoughts are often distressing ones. Try to structure the day so that you have time where distraction is naturally provided by other people - and try to make sure that they are people whose company tends to lift or relax, rather than stress or depress you.

Use some humour

This can come through trying to see something ridiculous in the situation that is distressing you or by distracting yourself with something funny, such as a film.

iv Self-help tool: Dealing with anger thoughts

We all know from experience that thinking anger thoughts winds us up to higher and higher levels of stress – up into the zone where our primitive security guard, rather than our rational brain, is beginning to seize control. It is likely that if we take action in this state it could well be damaging, both to others and ourselves. The following ABC model can be a useful way of stopping this from happening.[xiii]

A: Become **Aware** of anger thoughts that you are having. Separate yourself from them in some way: either label them with a big red anger label or give them a form – perhaps, like worry thoughts, seeing them as the 'enemy' trying to invade your rational thinking patterns.

B: **Block them.** Simply refuse to go there. Tell them where to go as forcefully as you can, or hold up a big 'Stop' sign in your imagination.

C: **Calm down**. Use some of your resource activities on page 56 that work with your system to distract your mind and calm it down. When this happens it will be possible to do one of two things:

• See that perhaps there is another way of looking at things: perhaps your partner meant to be helpful, not hurtful, and perhaps the guy on the other side of the bar always looks at people oddly and his glance was not directed particularly at you.

• Plan effectively (with your boss, the rational brain, in charge once again) to take steps to put right whatever has made you angry. This might be by seeking support with the difficulties you are having with your benefits, rather than sitting at home becoming increasingly angry about the situation (and possibly eventually getting so mad that you go to the benefits office and shout at someone), or by taking action to oil the squeaking gate that kept you awake last night (rather than stewing on it for hours until you become so frustrated that you rip the darn thing off its hinges).

v Holding on to anger

Sometimes, when discussing with a client how to take back control of their life and how to stop anger thoughts disrupting their waking hours and balance of sleep, it becomes apparent that there is something that makes them want to keep the anger alive. Perhaps the person, people or organisation with whom they are angry has done something so dreadful, and in their eyes so unforgivable, that to stop being angry would be to somehow say that it was all right, or to make light of the offence. If this applies to you, then it can be worth asking yourself a couple more questions before deciding whether you still want anger to be an active part of your life.

• On a daily basis, who is the anger impacting on most? You or them?

• On a nightly basis, whose sleep is anger damaging most? Yours or theirs?

You don't have to forgive them or 'let go' of your anger. Just not letting it actively damage your daily life and rest any longer is more than enough.

vi Guilt, shame and blame

*"It would be impossible to put into words the level of self-loathing
I used to feel. I hated what I had done; who I had become." JP*

As our stress levels rise and our brain changes from one that is calm and rational, with all our intelligence at its disposal, to one that is ruled by our primitive and far less intelligent security guard (amygdala), our thinking becomes more and more simplistic and is often called 'black and white' thinking. This is a thinking style that many people experiencing high levels of stress (be that due to PTS, anxiety or depression) recognise in themselves.

Many of the questions and considerations that arise around the issues of guilt, shame and blame are very complex and, quite simply, our security guard does not have the intelligence to deal with them fairly or effectively. This can lead to us feeling that we are completely to blame for a particular incident, or overwhelmed by guilt as the black and white thinking of our security guard is applied to issues that are perhaps, in reality, many shades of grey.

If you notice yourself thinking such thoughts when you are distressed, or if such thoughts cause your stress levels to rise, it can be useful to simply make an agreement with yourself that you will put them to one side for the moment, and focus on getting your system to a point (perhaps weeks or months down the line), where it is calm enough for your real intelligence (the boss) to get a look at them, and make a balanced and informed judgement.

If you do this, not only can a more accurate assessment be made, but you will be in a position to find intelligent ways to live with that judgement, or to make reparation should that be necessary.

vii Adding structure to the day

"Sometimes I spend so long trying to work out what to do that I don't end up getting anything done at all. And I don't really want to do any of it anyway. I just can't get myself going these days." JP

One of the most horrid things about low mood and depression is that it not only gradually shuts down our life, but it also takes away the desire to do the things that would lift the depression. It leaves us wallowing in a pit of despair where every task performed is an act of sheer willpower, and every day can be like wading through dark, sticky mud.

The brutal truth I have to tell my clients is that the biggest mistake they can make is to wait for those feelings of motivation to return before they start ironing their clothes, getting out for a walk, going to the gym. Somehow they have to begin to do the things that will make them feel better, even if their exhausted mind is screaming at them to just pull the duvet back up and hide from the world or continue the fruitless search for sleep that refreshes.

Because if someone does make the huge effort that it takes to get out and walk the dog, for example, not only does it reward with the benefits of fresh air, natural light and exercise (all covered in detail in Step 7), but it also, because of the outside stimulus of their environment and the naturally calming effect of the exercise, may give their mind a little bit of a break from the spinning thoughts.

And if, that day, they spend even an hour less worrying, and have even one thing that they can feel proud of having achieved (not therefore generating the emotional arousal that needs to be dreamed out of the system), their sleep has a chance to improve that very night, and it could be that the next morning they awaken a little more refreshed, with more motivation. That snowball effect again . . .

viii Self-help tool: Three safe things

> *"It may sound stupid but if I've had a shave I feel*
> *like I can face the world a bit better." AB*

Many of the veterans I have worked with have, either through the work we have done together or through their own understanding of what helps them to feel better, established a set of activities that they will do each day as a base line of ensuring that life continues to function even if they are feeling low.

These three things vary from person to person but often include something along the lines of the following:

• Getting dressed/washed/shaved. (A basic level of being 'presentable'.)

• Eating a 'proper' meal, however small, once a day.

• Walking the dog/walking to the shops.

• Washing the dishes.

• Doing one small thing for their partner or someone else.

• Going to the gym/for a run/for a swim/for a cycle.

Exercise:
Spend a couple of minutes considering whether building 'three safe things' into your day as a baseline of functionality may help you as it has helped them. Make a list of what those three things might be. You will notice as you do so that every single one of these activities improves one of the areas on the Wheel of Life that you completed earlier in the book.

ix Self-help tool: Small, achievable goals

"Everything had gone wrong. Trying to do one thing seemed pointless against the mess that life had become. Even the thought of it made me angry. But in the end it turned out that it worked." KB

When mood is low it is incredibly easy to become discouraged, to feel that you have failed, and that there is no point in even trying. Self-confidence can become very damaged in this way. In terms of moving forward and getting life to start moving in a positive direction, it is so important to build success back into it – however small to begin with.

If we set ourselves a hugely challenging goal, however – perhaps going from sitting in front of the TV for weeks on end, to suddenly deciding to do two hours of exercise every day, or from being completely reclusive to inviting several people around for a dinner party – we are probably setting ourselves up to fail, and this simply feeds the lies that depression tells us so convincingly: that we are inadequate and that even trying is pointless.

Small steps are often the quickest route to recovery. Set yourself something achievable, however small it may seem, and notice how achieving it – either as a one-off or consistently for the week – allows you to sense you have taken a step in a positive direction.

For one person a goal might be building 'three safe things' into their life each day. For another it might be meeting a friend for a cup of tea or calling someone with whom they had begun to lose contact. These small steps, insignificant as they may seem in the face of huge and seemingly overwhelming difficulties, have been, for many of those who I have worked with, the first steps on a journey back to life in the true sense of the word. A life where there is a sense that things are once again possible, and away from the bleak sense of impossibility and hopelessness that low mood lies to us is the case every morning on waking.

Step 5
Preparing to sleep well

"I'm having more nights now where I wake up in the morning feeling like I want to get up and I've slept well. That's a big change." SR

i Daytime preparations

Poor quality of sleep for any reason can leave us struggling to cope. When it is the result of daily stressors and terrifying dreams, the impact, as anyone who has developed a problematic post-traumatic response will know, can be devastating. Exhaustion is overwhelming. It is no coincidence that sleep deprivation is one of the most effective forms of psychological torture. It takes apart a person's mind. And yet when we suffer sleep deprivation due to emotional distress we sometimes underestimate the impact that it can have on our sense of self, and on our ability to cope and to think straight.

Doing all that we can to prepare to get a good night's sleep is therefore essential, and what we do during the day largely determines what quality of rest we will get at night.

First and foremost among these preparations – as by now will be clear – is dealing effectively with practical difficulties, and with anger and worry thoughts during daytime hours. If we can have fewer of these stressors in our life then, come bedtime, we will notice the benefits.

We can also, however, build up a good supply of the hormones and neurotransmitters involved in the process of going to, and then staying, asleep.

The two body/brain chemicals most closely linked to maintaining a healthy cycle of sleeping and waking are **serotonin** and **melatonin**.

Serotonin is a natural stimulant produced during the day, which regulates many of our body's natural systems, lifts our mood, and helps us to stay awake and alert during daylight hours. Serotonin levels are boosted naturally by vigorous exercise and exposure to natural light. (Levels of serotonin are boosted artificially by some medications.)

As dusk falls, our supply of serotonin is naturally converted into **melatonin** – also known as 'the sleep hormone'. If we have a good supply of serotonin built up during daylight hours this conversion happens more effectively.

Vigorous exercise and spending time out of doors in good natural light, particularly around mid-afternoon, can therefore directly improve the quality of our rest at night.

ii 'Winding down' time

Having made preparations for good sleep during the daytime, we can build on them in the evening by setting up a 'winding down time' before bed. This is a time when we 'draw a line' between daytime activities and night-time rest, and set up a pattern in our body and mind for settling down successfully.

Things to do in this winding down time might include:

• Turning the **lights down** lower. This kick-starts the production of our sleep hormone, melatonin.

• Having a **warm, milky drink**.

• Having a **relaxing bath or shower** before going to bed. Our body naturally cools as we drop off to sleep, and the change in temperature following a bath or shower can mimic this process.

• Being **physically close** to someone: hugging, gently stroking, massage. These activities all stimulate the release of oxytocin, a hormone which counters the effects of cortisol and increases feelings of 'safety' and 'trust', thereby smoothing the passage for sleep.

• Having **sex or masturbating**. Research shows that orgasms stimulate the release of the hormones associated with sleep.

• Getting lost in a good (but not too exciting!) book. **Reading**, especially in low light, which tires the eyes a little, can be an excellent way of settling the mind and body ready for rest.

• **Listening to a story CD or radio programme**. Occupying your thoughts in this way whilst being able to have the lights turned off can ensure that your mind has less chance to start racing or gravitating towards worries or frustrations. Many of the clients I work with find a book or story CD, read in a low, steady voice – rather than an edge-of-the duvet thriller, of course – is something that has transformed an endless and often fruitless quest for sleep into a more pleasant process of just drifting off.

• **Listening to a CD specifically designed to promote sleep and relaxation**

iii Creating a good environment for sleep

Practical preparations are also important in ensuring that we can settle down successfully and stay asleep effectively.

• Make sure that you will be **comfortable in bed**. (If possible, make sure you have a good mattress and pillow, and that you will be neither too hot nor cold.)

• Put up **blackout curtains** or blinds if the light wakes you – especially in the summer months.

• Wear **earplugs** if noises disturb you. (Many veterans find this hard, as they feel – both through the training that they have received and the hyper-vigilance that goes with PTS – that they need to remain aware in this way. If this is the case then some gentle background noise, relaxing music, a story CD or suchlike, can mask every tap of the radiators cooling, creak of the floorboards or sound outside which might otherwise disturb.)

• Make sure that the bedroom is kept primarily as **a place reserved for rest**. If you have a pile of unsorted paperwork or a heap of ironing or washing nagging at you from a corner then it is unlikely that you will be able to 'switch off' effectively.

iv Things to avoid

Just as some things promote good sleep, others make it more difficult to come by and are worth avoiding. These include:

• **Caffeine** during the late afternoon and evening. We all know that a good strong cup of coffee in the morning wakes us up. Unfortunately that's just what it will do to us late at night, too – wake us up just in time for bedtime! It is now known that caffeine, whether in the form of coffee or fizzy drinks such as cola, can suppress the production of melatonin for up to ten hours while at the same time increasing the supply of adrenaline.

• Too many **sugary snacks** or **eating late in the evening.**

• Too much **alcohol**. Two or three drinks may get you off to sleep, but in the middle of the night, when the alcohol has metabolised, your body goes into withdrawal.

• **Exercise within two hours of bedtime**.

• **Irregular bedtimes/wake-up times**. Setting a regular time for going to bed and a regular time when you will get up each day can begin to regulate your sleep cycle again if it has gone awry.

• **Late night news** programmes or phone calls that are likely to be stressful. Anything that stirs up our emotions during the evening is likely to make it far harder to settle.

• **Exciting or highly stimulating input** during your winding down time. Watching or listening to anything that is likely to 'wire' you up, such as distressing or exciting programmes on TV or music with a loud, fast beat.

• **Napping in the late afternoon or evening**. If you have a long nap late on in the day, you won't be ready for sleep come bed-time.

Exercise:
Write down a minimum of three things identified from the list above that would begin to improve the quality of your rest right away. The sooner you are able to awaken feeling refreshed the more manageable *everything* becomes.

Step 6
Developing coping strategies that work

"I was drinking to escape from it all, but every time I sobered up it was still there – and the rest of my life was falling apart even more." MH

i Addressing self-medication

Many people have, over the years, self-medicated with drink or drugs to blot out the pain and terror of a post-traumatic stress reaction and to gain a few hours of peace. This strategy is entirely understandable to anyone who has even a slight knowledge of how difficult living in a traumatised state can be.

The hard truth is, however, that almost every person I work with who has tried such coping strategies has confirmed that the price tag attached to any temporary escape, or 'forgetting', is very high, and that it has only led to further distress in their lives – sometimes pushing them into homelessness, debt or criminality.

But, a bit like trying to stop anger or worry thoughts, if we focus only on 'not self-medicating' we simply leave a huge need for a coping strategy in our life – which leads to more distress and makes us more likely to return to whatever tried, tested but damaging thing we have used so far.

If these faulty coping strategies have become major problems in their own right, and you are struggling with addiction, then getting support for this is a key part of recovery. A book that I would highly recommend is *Freedom from Addiction,*[xiv] which will not only clarify the science behind addiction (using language and characters you are familiar with from this book – and, yes, that security guard is a key player again), but will also point you to ways of moving forward and to appropriate sources of support.

Anything that is going to help us to really cope must work to counter the distressing symptoms of PTS directly. Something that:

• allows our system to calm down and thus lowers levels of cortisol and adrenaline.

• keeps our rational brain in charge.

• keeps us as far as possible from the symptoms of fight-or-flight.

• stops distressing thoughts during the day disrupting our sleep at night.

• contributes to good and restful sleep.

And these coping strategies, if you look back through the exercises you have undertaken during Part 2 of this book, are things that you now have:

7/11 breathing

Exercise

Pleasurable/distraction activities

Whenever you are considering using something as a coping strategy – and because different things work for different people (one person's sewing is another person's motorbike, as it were) – just check it out against the criteria above. If it ticks the boxes then it can safely be added to your list of things that will help you move towards a better quality of life.

ii Preparing to use your resources

In terms of preparing for difficult or dangerous situations, military personnel know more than most. Training repeatedly to perfect certain procedures and operations, in readiness for the time when they are needed, is second nature.

Training to use your resources in the fight to recover from PTS is just the same.

In order to develop and be able to use reliable and effective coping strategies:

• you need to know what resources you have at your disposal and have planned and practised how to use them: have a set of Standard Operating Procedures.

• you need a contingency plan if a situation escalates or an emergency arises and the first line of defence isn't quite enough.

• you may need to have some kind of written or physical reminder (such as a wristband/photograph or something else that you have attached a meaning to) just in case the boss is knocked out and the success of the operation is left in the hands of a primitive security guard – who simply doesn't have access to plans and coping strategies.

Bullet points of steps to take in an emergency can sometimes be enough to bring the boss round and begin calming the situation down. Sharing this with a trusted friend or relative so that they can remind you of what you can do to help yourself feel better can be of huge help too.

iii The power of positive imagining

Anyone who has any experience of the symptoms of PTS will understand only too well how powerful the imagination can be. It is our 'internal reality generator' and when things have gone awry, as happens in trauma, it can make us believe very powerfully that imagined things are real.

What is often forgotten, however, is that it is also one of our most useful tools – when we learn to use it effectively.

Many of the clients that I and my colleagues work with now use their imaginations in helpful rather than harmful ways, to set up pathways for new and effective ways of doing things. They imagine themselves dealing calmly with situations that in the past have caused distress – calming down swiftly when they notice anger building; feeling confident and in control.

Because we now understand that when we strongly imagine something, we create the same pathways in the brain as when we actually do it (and that the more we use a particular pathway the stronger it becomes). We can use our imagination to build patterns for new and helpful behaviour into our lives that will then be easier to follow in reality. Sports people use this understanding all the time to help them perform to the best of their ability.

If you are aware that until now your imagination has largely been out of control, and has been terrifying and distressing you on a regular basis, perhaps begin to experiment with using it to help you move forward. One of the truths about PTS is that having a good imagination is one of the pre-disposing factors for developing it. The good news is that this means that you almost certainly have an excellent tool at your disposal – once you begin to use it correctly.

A good therapist will tap into this knowledge and understanding, and will use this as a key part of the support that they offer. I make a recording for almost every client that I work with, guiding them through a process of using their imagination in a positive way, and promoting feelings of calm and deep relaxation. The vast majority find that this helps them to lower arousal levels, to begin to think clearly – and even to get to sleep.

Exercise:
Perhaps begin by noticing how much time you spend imagining things going wrong – imagining the 'worst possible outcome' in glorious detail. Just be aware of the utter hell you have been putting yourself through now that you know that the brain can't differentiate in neurological terms between a strongly imagined event and a real one!

How many bereavements has your system suffered, how many catastrophes has it been through, how many affairs has your partner had, how many times has there been a car accident or rail crash when someone is late?

Begin to harness that ability. Make it work for you. If you have made a plan that you are going to, for example, begin getting out for a walk with the dog each day, set up a pathway for that happening. When you have a quiet moment imagine yourself getting your coat on, getting the lead, opening the door, stepping outside. Imagine your arms swinging by your sides, each step you take feeling good. Imagine your return to the house afterwards, the reward of a cup of tea, a piece of cake.

Use your imagination to make it more likely that you will succeed in your endeavour to take these steps towards a better quality of life, rather than to terrify you out of trying.

Step 7
Building a healthier lifestyle

There are three key elements in building a healthier lifestyle:

Sleep   Exercise   Diet

The huge importance of sleep has already been covered in Step 5, and so here the focus is on the other two.

From the Wheel of Life that you completed earlier you will have a good idea of how these things look in your life at the moment. As I hope is now clear from this book, our body and mind are entirely linked together and so looking at our emotional good health in a holistic way, rather than simply dealing with individual problems in isolation, is by far the most effective way forward.

i Physical Exercise

Physical exercise in sensible amounts is extremely good for the mind. I always encourage clients to try to build it into their lives in some form or another, and the results are always positive. The simple fact is that, like everything else in this book, it is working in line with the science of our physiology. Exercise will:

• Boost **endorphins**. These are natural peptide chemicals produced in your body that interact with receptors in your brain. Healthy levels help you to feel focused, raise the pain threshold and improve mood. In a nutshell, endorphins promote a sense of well-being. On the other hand lower levels of endorphins are associated with increased awareness of physical pain and emotional distress.

• Focus **away from difficulties**.

• Build up our supply of **serotonin**. This neurotransmitter is a natural mood stabiliser, and it also converts into melatonin – the sleep hormone – which regulates sleep. Low levels of serotonin are associated with depression and anxiety. Two key ways of naturally boosting serotonin, without the need for prescription drugs and their inevitable side effects, are through exercise and exposure to natural light. A brisk walk in the fresh air ticks both boxes.

• **'Mop up' excess stress hormones** from a fight-or-flight response 'all dressed up with no-where to go', and thus help our rational brain, 'the boss', to remain in charge.

• **Improve sleep**.

For all the above reasons, physical exercise can leave you feeling calmer, steadier and thinking more clearly. It is also an important part of preparing for a good night's sleep and creates a sense of achievement – something you will feel good about having accomplished.

It is generally suggested that adults do 150 minutes of moderate exercise each week – equating to just over 20 minutes each day. Although this might sound like a lot if you have got out of the habit of being active, any exercise is better than none, and building up to a reasonable amount through small, achievable goals, is the best way to make it sustainable. And although some people benefit from a high-intensity workout, moderate exercise actually means doing something that makes you breathe a little faster and raises your heart rate but does not leave you out of breath.

Exercise:
Is physical exercise something that is already a part of the plan you are developing in beginning to address the symptoms of PTS? If not, then how could you build in this essential ingredient? Is there something that you have always wanted to have a go at doing? Is there an activity that you used to enjoy that perhaps low mood has persuaded you to phase out of your life?

ii A healthier diet

As scientific knowledge improves all the time so does our understanding of the fact that the fuel that we put into our body can directly affect not only our physical health, but also our emotional wellbeing. But it is very easy when things are tough, and when facing the appetite disturbances that often go hand in hand with so many forms of emotional distress, to let all thought of a 'healthy diet' fall by the wayside.

There is plenty of good information out there about what a healthy, balanced diet looks like – a diet, which in order to promote good mental health, would include:

• fresh vegetables and fruit.

• whole foods, such as grains and beans.

• eggs.

• oily fish.

But there are also some key areas worth highlighting when trying to improve and support our emotional wellbeing.

Sugar

One of the most common dietary issues that can seriously affect emotional health is blood sugar imbalance. This means the peaks and troughs caused by the fall and rise of our blood sugar – which drags our mood along in its wake.

If you tend to crave sweet food and lots of carbohydrates, or stimulants such as tea, coffee, or nicotine, it is likely that your system is being affected by this. Eating small regular meals, avoiding sugar itself, along with white processed foods and especially wheat-based products (wheat has more of an effect on blood sugar peaks and troughs than sugar itself), can lead to a steadying of the blood sugar and increased mood stability.

Omega oils

Omega oils are involved in the effective release of neurotransmitters such as serotonin. Without enough of this high grade oil, the brain has to rely on lower grade fats and simply does not function as effectively: it's a little like sticking vegetable oil in your Porsche. For this reason people whose diet is low in omega oils are more prone to depression, as the essential brain chemicals that lift mood simply cannot do their job as efficiently. Omega oils are found in seeds, nuts and oily fish such as herring, mackerel and salmon. If you know that your diet is lacking in these then taking a good quality supplement can be very helpful in lifting mood.

Making some small changes to a diet in line with this advice can be a very important part of the whole picture of recovery from trauma. Not only can it support healthy brain function and physical well-being, but it can also give us the correct and steady levels of energy necessary to sustain any other changes that we may be striving to make in our lives. When our diet is poor – when the fuel we are feeding the furnace with is inadequate – it is no wonder that the flames are not very bright.

Reduce caffeine intake

Caffeine, in both coffee itself and drinks such as coke or energy drinks, is an addictive stimulant. Not only does it delay production of the sleep hormone melatonin for up to ten hours (meaning that any coffee or energy drink after lunchtime is in all likelihood affecting your rest that night), but it also, through the withdrawal symptoms that can occur during the night, causes low mood, irritability and lack of energy which are often relieved only by – you guessed it!– a cup of coffee. It also dampens the brain's ability to be receptive to its own stimulant chemicals that give us a natural high with no side effects.

Exercise:
In the box below make a note of three things that you could do right away to improve your diet.

As with any changes, make these small, achievable steps – ones that can be built on once they are successfully in place. It could be something as simple as cutting back evening consumption of coffee, eating a piece of fruit at lunchtime or replacing white bread with wholemeal.

Step 8
Seeking psychological support

i When to seek support

It can be a huge step for many people to recognise that they need, and then actively to seek, support in the area of mental or emotional health. Whereas it is easy to go to a doctor and say, 'There seems to be something wrong with my knee', it is far harder to say, 'There seems to be something wrong with my mind.' This needs to change.

I recently began work with a member of the emergency services who, on entering into the room for our first consultation together, was so distressed that he couldn't remember his address and was struggling to speak at all for tears. I assumed this was caused by the trauma he had suffered, and the resultant symptoms. As things began to calm down (while we discussed everything from climbing to a mutual interest in the books of a particular author), he was finally in a position to explain that, although he was indeed suffering greatly because of 'what had happened', it was actually the realisation that 'I had got to the point where I needed to see a therapist' that was what had caused his extreme distress.

Happily, he is now well on the road to recovery – both from the experience of walking into a counselling room for the first time and from the legacy of the very distressing events he witnessed and was involved in as a paramedic.

If you are aware that the symptoms described in this book are really getting in the way of, or damaging, your quality of life then the best time to seek good support is sooner rather than later. It is perfectly possible to work back towards a really good quality of life again, where days can be pleasurable and nights restful and refreshing.

Therapy and counselling doesn't have to be a painful or lengthy process. In many of my sessions there is, believe it or not, alongside the tears and anger that occasionally arise, a lot of laughter as we begin to work through some very difficult subjects – with commonsense, practicality and a good dollop of real, scientific understanding in the pursuit of making sure that a life gets back on the right track as swiftly as possible. Dealing with even the most acute trauma memories need not involve lengthy revisiting or talking about the event or events – with the inevitable distress this so often causes – but can be done in a controlled and focused manner, working in line with our knowledge of how to calm down rather than stir up emotional arousal.[xv] Unfortunately this is not how many people experience counselling. This, too, needs to change.

A client who recently came through one of the organisations that I work with wrote the following, which I have included as an example of the doubts that exist for many when beginning to engage with professional help in this way. This is what is possible when the right support is combined with the right understanding:

"My initial thoughts were very sceptical, passed to another health care professional who was no doubt severely unfamiliar with the realities that conflict can instil on others. I dreaded the thought of watching their face as I disclosed my intrusive thoughts due to my personal experiences as a trauma medic. Their subconscious and impulsive reactions would surely display their disgust with my on-going battle within the confinements of my own brain.

Thankfully, I was paired with a very experienced psychotherapist. We quickly developed an excellent collaborative therapeutic relationship, identifying the areas that were causing concerns for me, and working together to locate suitable and effective strategies to combat the anxiety and difficulties I was facing around these incidences in Iraq – even working on other areas from early life which I still found difficult.

I was provided with a comprehensive supporting package throughout my treatment. Contact numbers, emails and even access to informative reading material were made available, and I found this very comforting. I personally believe that this support went above and beyond to ensure that I have all the necessary tools and support available to assist with a permanent recovery and now I actually enjoy the challenges that lie ahead."

– Former combat medical technician, Gulf veteran.

ii Where to find help

There are many excellent sources of support for individuals suffering from PTS, but at times they can be hard to find. Of course, as with any specialist skill that we need to bring into our lives, a word-of-mouth recommendation, or the evidence we see of a job having been done well, is probably the most desirable way to find someone with a proven track record.

In order to ensure the best possible outcomes, however, I have included below an Effective Counselling Checklist which anyone seeking support for themselves or a loved one should bear in mind.

This list does not apply to any one particular model of psychotherapy or counselling, but simply outlines what any therapy or counselling that works well should look like.

An effective psychotherapist or counsellor:[xvi]

• Knows how to build rapport quickly with distressed people.

• Understands depression and how to lift it.

• Helps immediately with anxiety problems, including trauma or fear related symptoms.

• Is prepared to give advice if needed or asked for.

• Will not use jargon or 'psychobabble', or tell you that counselling or psychotherapy has to be 'painful'.

• Will not dwell unduly on the past.

• Will be supportive when difficult feelings emerge, but will not encourage people to get emotional beyond the normal need to 'let go' of any bottled up feelings.

• May assist you to develop your social skills so that your needs for affection, friendship, pleasure, intimacy and connection to the wider community etc. can be better fulfilled.

• Will help you to draw and build on your own resources (which may prove greater than you thought).

• Will be considerate of the effects of counselling on the people close to you.

• May teach you to relax deeply.

• May help you think about your problems in new and more empowering ways.

• Uses a wide range of techniques as appropriate.

• May ask you to do things between sessions.

• Will take as few sessions as possible.

• Will increase your self confidence and independence, and make sure you feel better after every consultation.

There are many excellent therapists who work in this way, but from personal experience I can recommend the Human Givens Institute as an organisation whose registered therapists all work in the ways detailed above, and in line with up-to-date understanding and techniques. Details and a register of therapists can be found at www.hgi.org.uk or they can be contacted on +44 (0)1323 811662.

For veterans, reservists and family members, PTSD Resolution is an organisation that provides this kind of specialist trauma support free at point of service, within days, locally, briefly and highly effectively. Details can be found at www.ptsdresolution.org or by ringing +44 (0)300 302 0551.

Some final thoughts . . .

The Four Fs

In Part One we looked in detail at the fight-or-flight response and how, when this essential and natural survival mechanism is persistently and inappropriately fired and maintained due to a traumatic event or series of events, it can cause immense distress and a whole range of symptoms. We also touched on the third state in which we sometimes experience trauma if we can take no action to survive: Freeze. We established that if we *do* experience a trauma while in Freeze it is more likely that we will go on to develop a Post Traumatic Stress Reaction.

As you will now know, these Three Fs (Fight, Flight or Freeze) are all driven by our powerful but primitive subconscious brain – the bit presided over by the 'security guard'. They are automatic responses, not something that we 'decide' to do or are governed or controlled by rational thought.

In Part 2, we began to look at a fourth and perhaps less well known F. This fourth F is the one over which we have complete control. It stands for **FACE**, and is all about how we face the fact that we are suffering from Post-Traumatic Stress and how we begin to move on from the difficulties and symptoms associated with it.

This is the one F that our rational brain – the boss in the office – is in charge of.

We have complete control over:

- When we will choose to do this.

- How we will choose to do it.

- What information/support we will need to do so successfully.

There is no doubt that it can take real courage to begin to tackle this fourth F. My hope is that this guide will allow you to begin to see how you might do so – or to do so more successfully – and to make informed plans as to how you will continue with this task in the future.

A pattern for recovery

Recovery from Post Traumatic Stress, with the right understanding and support, is therefore absolutely possible.

In the past it has been a condition shrouded in confusion: a cluster of seemingly unrelated symptoms – from terror to anger, from nightmares to a dry mouth, from poor memory to alcoholism and depression – that have swept through a person's life and devastated it. I hope that this guide has removed some of that confusion and made clear that *all* these distressing symptoms are related to the fight-or-flight response being fired and maintained (or to the knock-on effects of this), and that any plan for recovery must work in line with this understanding.

Many of the veterans and other clients I see, even if they have been officially diagnosed as having a 'disorder' or being 'ill', begin to find it far more useful to see their difficulties and symptoms as a reaction to an extremely difficult event or events – as 'a hidden wound' or 'a psychological injury' – and to move towards recovery with the idea of recovering from 'injury' in mind.

When recovering from a knee injury, for example, you would expect to have to undertake a well-informed programme of exercise and rehabilitation. Sometimes expert advice – or a particular procedure to repair damage - might be needed too. *The same is true for PTS. Perhaps you might need to do daily exercises (such as 7/11 breathing) to strengthen your relaxation response. Perhaps it will take discipline to stick to this regime. Perhaps, too, you might need to talk to someone who understands what is going on.*

During rehabilitation, while making sure you exercised your knee to the right degree, you would probably be advised to avoid extreme load-bearing or high impact activities – anything that placed a strain on the recovering area – to avoid setting yourself back. *The same is true for PTS. Stretching yourself healthily is an important part of recovering, but if you take on too many stressful activities too soon you may well set your recovery back.*

If, in the early days of recovery from that knee injury, you were put in a position where you had to run down a long flight of stairs, or walk miles with a heavy pack, you would probably experience a flare up of symptoms or delay the healing process. *The same is true for PTS. If you suddenly find yourself dealing with a difficult situation, such as the loss of a relationship, an illness, a major life change or unexpected difficulty, it will be natural for symptoms to flare up a little, for a while.*

It could be that in the long term, even with expert support, exercises and rehabilitation, the damaged area might continue to flare up occasionally – especially if you chose, or were forced, to place strain upon it. In time, you would come to recognise patterns for this, and perhaps find ways of working around the injury or accept, without becoming distressed, that certain activities will have a 'price-tag' attached. *The same is true for PTS. When we can see this pattern, accept that it may happen and that any resultant symptoms will pass, any distress we experience from time to time becomes far more manageable and short-lived.*

And finally, it could even be that while recovering from your knee injury, while visiting the gym or walking to build up strength, while sitting in a waiting room or resting on a bench, you may discover places or people that you come to value within your life, and would not wish to be without. *The same, for some people, turns out to be true for PTS.*

Appendix

The rewind technique

The rewind technique is a non-intrusive, safe and highly effective psychological method for de-traumatising people, which can also be used for removing phobias. It should be carried out by an experienced practitioner and is only performed once a person is in a state of deep relaxation. (This ensures that the rational brain, the boss, is fully in charge.)

When they are fully relaxed, they are encouraged to bring their anxiety to the surface and then are calmed down again by being guided to recall or imagine a place where they feel totally safe and at ease.

Their relaxed state is then deepened and they are asked to imagine that, in their special safe place, they have a TV set and a video player with a remote control facility. They are asked to imagine floating to one side, out of body, and to watch themselves watching the screen, without actually seeing the picture (creating a double dissociation). They watch themselves watching a 'film' of the traumatic event that is still affecting them. The film begins at a point before the trauma occurred and ends at a point at which the trauma is over and they feel safe again.

They are then asked, in their imagination, to float back into their body and experience themselves going swiftly backwards through the trauma, from safe point to safe point, as if they were a character in a video that is being rewound. Then they watch the same images but as if on the TV screen while pressing the fast forward button (dissociation).

Because the 'double dissociation' and ordering the events backwards are complex procedures, the only bit of the brain capable of doing all of this is 'the boss', which means that as the memory is looked at he remains in charge, without the emotional responses of the security guard (amygdala) getting in the way – possibly for the first time. This allows communication between the rational brain and the amygdala to open up, allowing context and time to be added to the memory, meaning that it can take its rightful place in our narrative history as something very unpleasant but that happened 'back then' in a specific set of circumstances rather than, as happens when an untreated trauma memory is recalled, experienced as if it were still 'now'.

All this is repeated back and forth, at whatever speed feels comfortable, and as many times as needed, till the scenes evoke no emotion from the client.

If the feared circumstance is one that will be confronted again in the future -- for instance, driving a car or using a lift -- the person is asked, while still relaxed, to see themselves doing so confidently.

Besides being safe, quick and painless, the technique has the advantage of being non-voyeuristic. Intimate details do not have to be shared with the therapist [xvii].

Footnotes

i Ratey, J (2001) *A User's Guide to the Brain*. Little, Brown and Company, New York, London

ii Based on an idea by Mike Beard, REM State Consulting

iii For more information on the 'Freeze' state see *Waking The Tiger*, P. Levine (1997, North Atlantic Books

iv Griffin,J., Tyrrell,I., (2003) *A New Approach to Emotional Health and Clear Thinking*, Human Givens Publishing

v Adapted from *How to Master Anxiety*, Joe Griffin and Ivan Tyrrell. Human Givens Publishing

vi Griffin, J., Tyrrell, I., (2003) *Dreaming Reality*, Human Givens Publishing

vii For a full explanation of the links between dreaming sleep and depression see *How to Lift Depression . . . Fast*, Joe Griffin and Ivan Tyrrell, Human Givens Publishing. For further information on dreaming sleep see *Why We Dream*, Joe Griffin, Human Givens Publishing

viii Adapted from Beck, A., Emery, G. and Greenberg, R.(1985) *Anxiety Disorders and Phobias*. Basic Books

ix Hendon, J., (2001) *Beating Combat Stress: 101 Techniques for Recovery*, Wiley

x Adapted from the work of Babette Rothschild

xi Based on The Emotional Needs Audit devised by Joe Griffin and Ivan Tyrrell

xii Griffin, J., Tyrrell, I., *How to Lift Depression . . . Fast*, Human Givens Publishing

xiii Griffin, J., Tyrrell, I., *Release from Anger*, Human Givens Publishing

xiv Griffin, J., Tyrrell, I., *Freedom From Addiction*, Human Givens Publishing

xv The Rewind Technique: see Appendix, page 118

xvi Effective Counselling Checklist: The Human Givens Institute, www.hgi.org.uk

xvii The outline of the Rewind Technique is adapted from The Human Givens website, where further information regarding this technique and comparison with other approaches to trauma work can be found.

Further reading

A User's Guide To The Brain: John Ratey, Little Brown publishing

How to Lift Depression . . . Fast: Joe Griffin and Ivan Tyrrell, Human Givens Publishing

Mastering Anxiety: Joe Griffin and Ivan Tyrrell, Human Givens Publishing

Release From Anger: Joe Griffin and Ivan Tyrrell, Human Givens Publishing

Dreaming Reality: Joe Griffin and Ivan Tyrrell, Human Givens Publishing

Waking The Tiger: P. Levine, North Atlantic Books

Beating Combat Stress: 101 techniques for Recovery, John Hendon, Wiley

Afterword

by *Major General Andrew Keeling CB CBE*,
Former Commandant General, Royal Marines

In his foreword Gordon Turnbull concludes that he hopes that this book will be widely read by survivors and therapists, and that it will help to eradicate the hidden enemy – *stigma*. I am neither a survivor nor a therapist, but I am a former Cold War era Royal Marine who, in the aftermath of the Falklands War in 1982, for the first time heard the initials PTSD being used. All of a sudden the suggestion then was that it was likely a small percentage of those who had been exposed to shocking traumatic events would suffer psychologically, and that their suffering was likely to be debilitating and potentially fatal.

Royal Marines training was, and remains, physically tough and very demanding. Endless PT sessions and long marches and exercises, often carrying heavy loads, are invariably accompanied by throw-away expressions such as 'It's only pain', and 'If you don't mind it doesn't matter' and 'There's no gain without pain' – and so on – from our well-meaning instructors. But years ago all reference to 'pain' concerned physical pain. No consideration was given to psychological pain, or the potential of mental injury resulting from a traumatic experience.

Recent wars in Iraq and Afghanistan have changed all that. PTSD is now widely acknowledged in the military, and all ranks are trained, to some extent at least, to appreciate that it does exist, to anticipate it and recognise it, and if necessary to accept it. We have learned that PTSD does not respect rank or age or background or experience. I know several highly professional, seriously physically tough, intelligent, well-trained and successful people who have been struck down by it. It is a frightening, debilitating, unpredictable, confusing condition that seems to swamp and overwhelm the sufferer. It can strike quickly, but is more likely to take several years to present, and can take many years to manifest itself. I knew an old soldier who had horrific experiences in a Japanese Prisoner of War camp in World War 2, who eventually returned to England having lost his sight and both hands and weighing just five stone, but through determination and with much courage got his live together again. His PTSD developed when he was over 90 – nearly 70 years after the psychological damage was first done.

PTSD is now widely acknowledged, and effective treatment exists – but it is still a curse to those who have it, and often to those that live with those who have it. It is still potentially debilitating and destructive. But as this this excellent book by Rosalind Townsend explains, there is light at the end of the PTSD tunnel, for she does much to dispel the myths and gobbledygook that often accompanies diagnosis. I hope it will be widely read, and that it will add substantially to the help needed by all those affected directly or indirectly by this very real and unpleasant condition.

Major General Andrew Keeling CB CBE